FINANCIAL DI$TRACTION

Keep your receipt!

This book is tax deductible!

Also by Dr Steven J Enticott

Big V's Boutique

Tax Effective Investing

HOW TO DEAL WITH

FINANCIAL DI$TRACTION

DR STEVEN J ENTICOTT

First published 2013
Financial Distraction Pty Ltd
PO Box 2390 Moorabbin 3189

Cataloguing-in-Publication data is available at the National Library of Australia.

ISBN 978-0-646-55564-5

Edited by Richard Millership
Produced by End2End Books
Designed by Andrew Cunningham—Studio Pazzo
Typeset in Scala (10/15pt) by Studio Pazzo
Printed in Australia by McPherson's Printing Group

GENERAL ADVICE WARNING

The material contained in this publication is intended to provide a general commentary only, should not be regarded as specific, personal financial advice, is no substitute for personal financial advice, and has been prepared without taking into account any individual's personal objectives, financial situation, or needs. In addition, anyone considering acquiring a financial product should always obtain a Product Disclosure Statement and consider its contents before making any decisions. Always consider the information in this publication in light of your personal objectives, financial situation or needs, and always consult a licensed financial advisor before taking action.

This book was written in 2013 specifically for Australian Tax Residents, and tax rates used were current at the time of writing. As this book is a general guide, and does not cover all the intricacies of Australian tax law, all calculations and marginal tax rates used have been simplified to reflect an average overview, and are not exact and do not contain, for example, items like Medicare Levy Surcharges or Tax Rebates. As a result, specific tax advice will always be required.

Past and future capital growth rates used are educated assumptions not necessarily based on historical performance, nor can anyone can guess at or guarantee the future performance of any asset class.

Interest rates used in calculations of income and expenses were an approximation of rates current at the time of writing.

This book is intended to be an aid to starting the process, to educate, and to provide ideas and thoughts that can be worked through with a professional advisor (tax, law, financial, accounting, etc) before taking any kind of action. Dr Steven Enticott, CIA tax/wealth, its principals, agents and staff assumes no responsibility for any actions you take independently.

DEDICATION

This book, believe it or not, is actually a work of love (well my attempt at it anyway) written to ease and remove niggling and sometimes crushing financial distractions from your life through the use of mostly real-life case study examples stemming from sixteen years of experience in public accounting and six concurrent years of financial advising, and is therefore a dedication to the many people I have worked with over that time.

Ultimately, this book is a dedication to my faith and to the loving creator of life.

ACKNOWLEDGEMENTS

Richard Millership is the very fine editor of this work and an author in his own right. Richard points out that my writing can occasionally get a little too busy getting points across to worry about the prose. The points made throughout this book are made readable through Richard's highly credentialed interpretive ability and penmanship, both of which are gratefully acknowledged.

ABOUT THE AUTHOR

Dr Steven J. Enticott is the Senior Partner and founder (1999) of CIA Tax (www.ciatax.com.au), a personal tax-based business and investment practice.

Being an independent licensed financial advisor (DiPFS) specialising in tax-effective investment, as well as having a noteworthy academic background in related fields (comprising a Doctorate, an MBA and several Diplomas), Dr Enticott has a unique ability to communicate complex financial concepts in clear and practical ways that everyone can understand.

There are few members of this industry that are able to provide holistic financial advice. By combining a successful accountancy career and broad finance-industry experience with the academic rigour required for significant further study in the field of finance, not to mention being a fiercely independent financial advisor, has successfully provided Dr Enticott with the critical qualities needed to effectively write about successful financial management.

While successful financial management and money making come naturally to some, it is a rare individual that can be a successful financial manager while also being able to relate to a client, understand their often complex financial affairs as well as their goals and dreams, and express it all simply and efficiently, and in way that will enable them to make their dreams come true.

CONTENTS

FOREWORD

In *Financial Distraction* Dr Steven Enticott delivers the recipe for financial freedom and independence. As Steve says, he has written the book as a work of love – coupling his unbridled optimism with a big dose of care and attention to the details that can radically help (or hinder, if they are ignored) everyday Australians. Having known and engaged professionally with Steve for over a decade, it's unsurprising that he combines this passion and care for the individual, along with the precision of a dedicated tax and accounting professional. The word "love" is one that Steve uses a lot – and he really means it!

When I first heard that Steve was writing this book, it struck me that Australia is ready for this type of "self-help" manual. Where once we lived in an uncomplicated and growing country with unbounded opportunity and appropriate time for leisure, we are now faced with complexity most everywhere we look. We work longer hours than ever before, striving to get ahead quicker and better than our parents did. We place our financial faith in owning our own home, and rapidly accumulate levels of debt that our parents would never have dreamed of. Most of us have the benefit of compulsory superannuation – but the modest returns that are typical from mainstream superannuation providers (coupled with the disgrace that was the GFC) means that personal financial freedom is something that may be a long way off for many of us. And as Steve highlights, adversity like divorce, ill health and the "hard yards" that are typical for most of us in small business, can make it really hard to get ahead in life.

The big difference in Financial Distraction is that Steve writes from the perspective of years of practical experience – formed with his passion for knowledge and higher learning and with Steve's love of humankind clearly in evidence on every page. How many suburban accountants do you know that have a Doctorate? (And a Doctorate focusing on financial derivatives, to boot!) So when Steve sets outs his recipe for overcoming the financial distractions that prevent so many of us from living a life of financial freedom, he clearly does so with technical credibility and accuracy.

That's something that deserves a little more comment. For most Australians, the first step they take towards financial freedom leads to a trip to the local financial planner or accountant. As Steve says in his book, there are many caring and literate financial planners and accountants in Australia. In my experience as a trainer and consultant to the financial planning industry, I can certainly attest to that – and may your search for an adviser lead you to one of the "good guys." Armed with Financial Distraction as your guide, you may well find a good adviser (or do it yourself) – but beware of the pitfalls that surround the typical financial adviser or accountant.

The problem is that the major institutions that own most financial advisory firms, and the researchers and "asset consultants" that are the backbone of the independent boutique financial advisory businesses, live in a textbook world that is almost completely out of synch with our modern reality. Investment returns are measured by these "professionals" in what are cryptically referenced against "rolling 7-year periods" – a way of looking at average returns over a very long period of time. Large wholesale investment management systems are "blind" to the specific needs and aspirations of individuals – so they justify their existence based on how their returns compare to long-term averages.

The irrelevance of the traditional approach was highlighted by the GFC – where even the world's best "diversified" portfolios (ie, professionally designed and constructed according to the rules of the "rolling 7-year returns" approach) fell by up to 50%. Five years later, most of these professionally designed portfolios are still way below their pre-GFC values.

A minority of professional investment managers and financial advisers have re-booted to try to overcome these problems, but for most it's business as usual. The problem has started to become publicized and politicized, with ex Treasury Secretary Ken Henry making public his criticism of the traditional approach in 2012,when he highlighted the problem he calls "sequencing risk." What he means by that slogan is how bad/damaging a severe fall in asset prices can be to someone who is about to (or has) retired. Traditionally constructed portfolios – like the ones that typical financial advisers will prepare for you – assume that an investor can achieve "average" returns if they invest for a long enough period of time. Sequencing risk points out that a big market fall late in life will be very hard to overcome – there just isn't enough time or income to allow the portfolio value to rise to the level needed for a suitable retirement.

You won't find acknowledgment of these problems from a traditional financial adviser or accountant – and so it's vibrantly refreshing to read Financial Distraction – because Steve so candidly and openly shows you the tips and details of successful investing that he has accumulated over his professional life.

Financial Distraction highlights some of the usual methods for building financial prosperity – like starting early, sound budgeting, owning your own home, and utilizing superannuation – but then builds on Steve's "Three Pillars" approach to introduce the concepts of tax-effective investing. The chapters on "good debt" and "bad debt" are crucial for all Australians to understand – and for any parent of young adults moving into the crosshairs of our major lending institutions, showing them these chapters on the problems that debt can cause will be an important game changer.

Financial Distraction then moves onto some seriously good analysis of the benefits and pitfalls of property and share investing. It introduces concepts like low cost Exchange Traded Funds, share portfolio protection – and the great power of the "legal onshore tax haven" which our Self Managed Super Fund ("SMSF") provides. The chapters on investing are rounded out with easy to understand detail on farming in your SMSF, the use of trusts and estate planning ideas, and efficient structuring for small business owners.

Being grounded in the real world means that Steve also spends some time in his book, on the issues around financial recovery from divorce. If half of all marriages end up in divorce, this material must be highly relevant for many Australians.

Through all of Financial Distraction, Steve Enticott flavours his advice with the practical optimism that is his guiding philosophy: "Do Something – NEVER Do Nothing." For any Australian looking for a practical, easy to understand guide to achieving financial freedom (and based on a technically highly accurate approach), Financial Distraction is a must read.

Tony Rumble, PhD
Founder, ASX Listed Products Accreditation Course
("LPAC Online")

INTRODUCTION

Life is challenge. And one of life's greatest challenges comes from financial distraction.

This entire story – my story, your story – is about learning to ensure financial distractions do not stop you from living your life to the fullest. This is because money, finance, and financial security can represent the greatest distractions you or I will ever face. And these things impact nearly everything we do. We need to change that. We need to be free. And the fact is that we really can be.

> **Simple fact:** the reasons people tell themselves why they have to work can be complex, not to mention often wrong.
>
> **Simple reality:** most of us work to live. This reality is why personal financial circumstances will always dictate why we work.
>
> **Simple life lesson:** our financial reality affects our work and life balance, as it must.
>
> **Moral:** life's financial imperative represents the most significant distraction you or I will ever face.

With the link between 'why we work' and 'financial distraction' established, it is of much greater benefit to not only eliminate distraction but also to align your financial goals with what you're currently doing in terms of how you earn your living.

By setting out to eliminate the financial distractions in your life, you set in train a process that will lead to much greater life engagement.

So, what are the major financial distractions we face in our lives? There are a number, but here are the most basic:

- **Standard of living**
- **Measures of worth**
- **Debts and credit**
- **Children (education/living)**
- **The effect of illness or death**
- **Divorce and separation**
- **Cash flow and budgeting**
- **Investments and taxes**
- **Retirement planning**

Putting it simply, eliminating financial distraction enables you to engage fully with your life. And when you are fully engaged with life, greater motivation, and even joy, will inevitably follow.

Why write this book?

No one can enjoy life to its fullest when they're financially distracted. This can often lead to huge personal costs. For example, a family breadwinner struggling to cope financially will be highly distracted. Naturally, many people in this situation will start trying to work longer hours, two or maybe three jobs, or try chasing down higher paying jobs, all of which represent sacrifices involving long working hours, excessive travel time, totally lost family time, and all in pursuit of a dream to finally – *finally* – be able to cope financially, and only to find all of that doesn't work either.

Sometimes the distractions we face are unconscious and even hearing me say something like that, you may still find it difficult to believe they exist. But the fact remains: when you scratch the surface, these distractions have always been there and they're dominating your life.

The news isn't all bad, though, and the answer to the problem is basic.

You fix it.

And this book, through its broad case studies, will start you off on the road to a life free of financial distraction.

My crusade

When I started to write this book, it started out as a crusade, and entirely in response to sitting down with thousands of people over the years, putting their affairs in order and into context while helping them to either fulfil their dreams, or to just extract the best they could from the cards they were dealt.

This often brings enormous relief, because in most cases people are already where they need to be, or are a matter of only a few steps away (only they're too distracted to see it).

This book represents the kind of thing that the financial planning industry should have been doing before it tarnished its good name by over-selling financial products with upfront commissions, trailing commissions, and overall poor returns. And I can say this, because I am both an accountant *and* a financial advisor.

While most financial planning professionals have a good heart and the best intentions, for many of them, commonsense got a little lost somewhere. Fortunately, the industry has started to rebuild its credibility, but it will take time to regain the community's trust.

The names and precise circumstances in the various case studies we are about to explore have been changed, of course, but the circumstances you're about to read about are all from real situations involving real people.

Before we take a small glimpse into the lives of others, though, and the methods I used to turn their lives around, I want to spend a few moments talking about my philosophy for a non-distracted financial life.

THE WHOLE POINT

Giving in to financial distraction means losing site of personal vision and failing to set realistic goals. With this simple definition in mind, each case study we examine will help to put each individual's circumstances into some context (some quite dire), but all of them will ultimately address this main theme.

Being attuned to your vision and realistic goals is the basis for eliminating financial distraction. The problem is that it's not that easy to align our visions and goals to our financial circumstances, especially when we're already on the *inside* 'looking in'.

Fitting your visions and goals within the passage of time, enabling you to stop slaving away at unrealistic objectives by setting new goals to achieve the same outcomes, is this book's primary objective.

Now, with this in mind, as you review the case studies and solutions, think about how each one aligns with your circumstances for a view from the *outside* looking in.

This is basically what I do whenever I take a client under my wing, and this is what I'm hoping my book will do for you, too.

PART ONE

USING POSITIVES

ETERNAL OPTIMIST

I want you to 'get' this book, and I want you to get the very most you can out of it. So I need to provide you with a little insight into the way I think and where my methods for eliminating financial distractions essentially come from. I thought it was important enough to include this additional introduction because it will help you to understand where the words stem from and how the thinking is applied.

Skip it if you like. Cut straight to the chase and head to the relevant case studies – The Lives of Others – but you might miss out on getting the full story, so bear with me.

My biggest problem and my inspiration

I admit it. I'm an eternal optimist. I can't help looking for the positive side in any situation.

Some of this optimism is natural and some of it stems from a strong spiritual belief, but a lot of it is learned and ultimately developed through reflection and practice. And then one day, a state of almost perpetual optimism takes over.

Some people find this overwhelmingly positive approach to life annoying, but let's face it, if you're reading this book you have an enormous bank of positives to draw from, and this is how we'll approach eliminating your financial distractions from this point on.

A lot of my thinking and methodologies are inspired by the work of a psychologist by the name of Martin Seligman and his exploration of the brave new world of Positive Psychologies, which I admit to significantly adapting through extensive personal experience in my chosen field (and others).

How does this work for you?

The most significant and irreplaceable positive in life is you. You have a lot to be positive about, because the act of living is actually a terrific talent.

Most of us think too much about what went wrong or *is* wrong in our lives, and not enough about what was or *is* going right, right now.

Seligman talks about this very issue and offers us a simple remedy, which comes from shifting focus and reminding ourselves daily of three positive things in our lives (try it yourself).

We can learn from Seligman.

Let's address the most common negatives.

Age and the passage of time

Age and ageing is the issue that crops up nearly every time I consult with a client (not to mention personally). We're all in a rush to get where we want to go. The problem is that we're so focussed that we completely fail to see where it is we actually are.

When we're young, we not only have endless energy, but we're also starting from our lowest point in terms of net wealth. If we're lucky enough to be in a relationship (double income no kids, or DINKs for short), money is almost literally pouring in the door and the growth we're experiencing, coming from this low net-wealth base as we are, is relatively easy and exciting to see. It's an amazingly motivating time of life.

If you're at this stage of your life, revel in it. It's a fabulous place to be! When you're young you've got the energy to advance: up late after work, renovating houses, boosting capital values, working overtime or even additional jobs, getting regular pay rises, or finding yourself with plenty of time for growing a business. You're building wealth relatively easily, feeding motivation and enthusiasm.

Then in a lot of cases, it suddenly all comes to a grinding halt.

People get married, some have children, and every parent can appreciate what happens next. Not only does the income fall, as one partner generally stops working, but costs rise significantly, and even though having children can be one of the greatest things that can happen, everyone's focus inevitably shifts and the wealth growth of our youth finally stops.

This situation doesn't apply to everyone, of course, and this book isn't intended to focus on any particular life-style type, but the fact remains: it doesn't have to be children that put a stop to the initial growth spurt in our wealth. Ill-health can be the cause of another major stunting of financial growth, both for you personally or for a family member or partner.

The strange thing about ill-health, though, and serious ill-health in particular, is that it too shifts your focus from the importance of things like financial security, to the thing that *really* matters and that's life itself. Assuming we pass through this phase, eventually financial security and growth becomes the distraction it has always been.

There are plenty of other life experiences that can bring things to a halt (divorce being one), but we'll focus on the financial distractions from the advance of time at this point.

So how do you work in some positives when it comes to the advance of time?

Let's start looking at some examples.

FORTY-SEVEN YEARS OLD...

... And well behind where I want or need to be. My career has stalled and the marriage is shaky because we're constantly arguing about money, given my partner never returned to serious paid work after the children.

Far from making any dents in the mortgage, it's actually rising slightly each year, what with the kids' secondary education to pay for on top of all the other demands on our single income.

To top it all off, my superannuation has been slaughtered, so there's no way I'll be retiring at 55, and with my nearly 70-year-old mother's chronic health issues and associated bills, where's that going to leave me and my retirement at 65, in just 18 years time?

This is a fairly typical situation and understandably represents a life full of financial distractions. So what's one way to respond to what will appear to most people to be a fairly bleak outlook?

Is my mortgage really a problem? After 18 years, the payments will fall as the balance falls, and even if it doesn't happen quite that way, inflation is still deflating the balance, 'shrinking' the real value of the mortgage, and inflating our property's price, creating a bigger gap between debt and equity, and all by doing absolutely nothing.

As for my superannuation, I can start treating it seriously and review the fees and the advisor commissions I'm paying. By taking an entirely new and sensible approach to my investment strategies, and with so much adding to it from my wages each month, over the next 18 years that balance will increase and compound in plenty of time.

My cost of living over the next six years will start to fall as the children finish secondary school and move onto university and out of home. Knowing this means I can stop being distracted by it and plan to maintain a neutral cash flow over that period, after which we'll have a solid base to grow from.

After that, and hopefully with my partner retrained and back into the work force full time, we'll return to a positive cash flow again, adding to superannuation with our property's value and mortgage gap growing steadily. With 12 years of this, and the ability to take on other investments, we're really looking like we're on track.

While planning to retire earlier may not be an option, reducing my hours to three days a week when I reach 55 certainly is.

And finally, what does it matter? A good friend got seriously ill recently, and one of the senior managers at work suffered a major heart attack. And when I think about that, I realise that none of these financial distraction really matter when it's all said and done. Spending time with family and friends is what really matters and that costs me nothing at all.

So what's the moral of this story about financial distractions due to the advance of time? It's simple. Relax. Do a balance sheet (with a professional, if you like) that focuses on the passage of time and take the pressure off yourself. Learn to enjoy your time no matter where you are.

Being ungrateful

It isn't all bad is it? Try taking a look at the things that have gone well with your life and be grateful for them. Make a list. Maybe a family member helped you with a house deposit, or a boss gave you employee shares that have grown significantly. It may have been a joint investment that a friend put you into or a stroke of luck at an auction you bid on that left you with an asset that has since taken off. Maybe it's an inheritance that came your way or just some other lucky break that's brought you to where you are now.

For whatever reason, we just don't take enough time to simply be grateful.

FIFTY-ONE YEARS OLD...

... And living in a great house with some equity, and entirely because our parents helped us with the deposit on a 'little renovator's delight' we spent countless hours on turning into the terrific asset it is today.

So, I was lucky enough to have met my life-partner after a first marriage that went bad, and we've stuck it out through the good times and the bad. Now we have a solid base that'll enable us to settle down in our twilight years, while so many of our friends have been divorced and lost what foundation for the future they'd managed to build.

While I married too young and divorced my first wife after only a few years, the children from that marriage have turned out just fine. I have had to change my goals and visions to suit my circumstances, but I'm still just so grateful that it worked out.

This is another common situation and a grateful outlook even in the face of adversity.

Here's another situation I've seen all too often:

> *I have nothing left. The business I spent the last 10 years building went broke, thanks to a major debtor that went down the tubes. But you know what? My health is great and I've found a new career that actually matches my passions and hobbies. I love what I'm doing everyday and hope to do it till I'm 80. In hindsight, I'm actually glad I went broke. What I'd been doing for the last 10 years was almost literally killing me.*

So what's the moral of this story about the financial distractions from being ungrateful? Take time to be grateful for what you have.

Some of my clients have faced some of the worst circumstances I can imagine, and yet they're most often the ones who are the most grateful for even the small good that life has dealt them (and I have to say, it's an amazingly infectious way of looking at life).

So make that list. In fact, go one step further and write a letter or make a gratitude visit to the people you are most grateful for in your life.

It's an amazing feeling when you do.

Being ashamed

It's not shameful to be satisfied with or proud of what you've achieved. Look back at where you started from, and compare it to the place you find yourself in today. Be positive. Not everything goes your way. Set-backs are normal, and it's simply not worth dwelling on them. The things that have gone your way, though, you should be very proud of indeed.

We need to take time to remember the things we can be proud about in our lives.

THIRTY-NINE YEARS OLD ...

... And I've got a Masters degree. I've worked my way into a great role with plenty of room to move on or up with the experience I'm getting.

... My kids are great, though trying at times, but making the sacrifices to put them through good private schools is one of my proudest achievements...

... My business didn't reach the dizzying heights I wanted it to, but it did darned well for the past decade. When you look at the statistics on how many business fail in the first few years, surviving a decade in great shape is one heck of an achievement...

... Taking a risk, against the advice of family and friends, and buying the house next door when it went up for auction really paid off. Now, with developers taking an active interest in the area, the sky is very blue indeed...

... Making the effort, when most don't even think about it, to consolidate all my superannuation into the one account, meant reducing fees and eliminating advisor commissions. Reviewing the fund's performance each year, along with my salary sacrifices and tax savings, has put me in a very secure position, and it's something I am really proud of...

Take time to be proud of what you've achieved.

Positive psychology

You were warned.

Being completely optimistic is an infectious way to look at life and in my case heavily influenced by positive psychology. Because when you think positively, positive things start to happen. Dwell on the negatives and it's another story altogether.

With this simple philosophy in mind, it's now time to pull back the curtain on our own lives before taking a longer, more detailed look into the lives of others.

PART TWO

HOW WE DO IT

YOUR FINANCIAL HEALTH

Step one

Let's start our journey with my Financial Health Index template. This index is something I developed from a number of different sources over the years, as a way of keeping track of a client's progress over time, and more importantly, as an advisor, to give me a checklist covering the main points I need to monitor. For example, for the question 'Do you have a budget?', if your answer is 'yes', then score 5 points in that column (and the score can vary, depending on the question). If your answer is 'no', then you get a big fat zero!

Now, over to you.

FINANCIAL HEALTH INDEX

www.ciatax.com.au

LIFESTYLE GOALS AND OBJECTIVES

	SCORE	PRESENT	20__	20__	20__	20__	20__
Q1. Have you clearly defined your lifestyle goals?	5						
Q2. Do you review these goals regularly?	5						
Q3. Do you have a definition of success you are working towards?	5						
Q4. Do you have financial advisers?	10						

(The five 20__ columns are headed "YEARS".)

CASH FLOW

	SCORE	PRESENT	20__	20__	20__	20__	20__
Q1. Do you have a budget?	5						
Q2. Do you review your budget regularly?	5						
Q3. Does your annual net cash flow meet your expectations?	5						

DEBT STRATEGIES

	SCORE	PRESENT	20__	20__	20__	20__	20__
Q1. Do you have non-tax deductible debt? eg. mortgage on principle place of residence, credit card.	-10						
Q2. Do you know when you will be debt free?	5						
Q3. Do you have any tax deductible debt? eg. investment loan for shares	10						

ASSET PROTECTION

	SCORE	PRESENT	20__	20__	20__	20__	20__
Q1. Do you have life insurance?	5						
Q2. Do you have disability insurance?	5						
Q3. Do you have income protection insurance?	5						
Q4. Do you have critical illness insurance?	5						
Q5. Do you have the minimum level required for the above insurance?	5						

ESTATE PLANNING

	SCORE	PRESENT	20__	20__	20__	20__	20__
Q1. Do you have a valid up to date Will?	5						
Q2. Do you have a Power of Attorney?	5						
Q3. Will income from the estate be tax effective for your dependants?	5						

FINANCIAL HEALTH INDEX

www.ciatax.com.au

SUPERANNUATION

	SCORE	PRESENT	20__	20__	20__	20__	20__
Q1. Do you have more than two superannuation funds?	-5	☐	☐	☐	☐	☐	☐
Q2. Are you aware of how much super you will have at retirement?	5	☐	☐	☐	☐	☐	☐
Q3. Are you contributing additional amounts to super for you or your spouse?	5	☐	☐	☐	☐	☐	☐
Q4. Do you fund insurance for death and disability via your super?	5	☐	☐	☐	☐	☐	☐
Q5. Do you pay a contribution fee?	-5	☐	☐	☐	☐	☐	☐
Q6. Have your personal super funds been reviewed in the last 12 months?	5	☐	☐	☐	☐	☐	☐

(YEARS)

INVESTMENTS

	SCORE	PRESENT	20__	20__	20__	20__	20__
Q1. Apart from your home and super do you have other investments?	10	☐	☐	☐	☐	☐	☐
Q2. Are your investments in line with your risk profile?	5	☐	☐	☐	☐	☐	☐
Q3. Do you rebalance your investments regularly in line with your risk profile?	5	☐	☐	☐	☐	☐	☐
Q4. Have you formally reviewed performance in the last 12 months?	10	☐	☐	☐	☐	☐	☐
Q5. Are your investments aligned to your lifestyle goals?	5	☐	☐	☐	☐	☐	☐
Q6. Are you diversified across all asset classes?	10	☐	☐	☐	☐	☐	☐
Q7. Are you investment returns in line with your expectations?	10	☐	☐	☐	☐	☐	☐

Total

Total Possible Score

Index = Total divided by 150 x 100 = %

TOTAL	☐	☐	☐	☐	☐	☐
MAX	150	150	150	150	150	150
INDEX	☐	☐	☐	☐	☐	☐

How did you go? Not so well? Now for the good news: your score is totally irrelevant. What really matters is identifying the things you need to address to remove financial distraction, along with providing a numerical measure to guide you as you improve your situation.

Step two

Once you've identified the financial distractions you haven't scored so well on, pick out the top two urgent issues (though I have to warn you at this point, *never* try to address all your issues at once, as it becomes overwhelming, and total inaction will very likely be the result).

At this point, try following an adaptation of Dale Carnegie's[1] three steps for eliminating worry.

1. **Think of the worst possible outcome.**
2. **Take personal responsibility for this.**
3. **Now work hard to improve it.**

An example

If you're an average kind of person, and you have dependents relying on your income, it's likely you're already facing the two most urgent financial distractions you need to address. Whether your dependents are your children, a spouse, handicapped siblings, or even a dearly loved pet or neighbour you support, it's likely that you have no Last Will and Testament in place and no life insurance to provide for them if the worst possible outcome occurs.

When we apply Carnegie's three rules to this scenario, we come up with the first step: thinking of the obvious worst outcome, which is your death (or worse, permanent incapacitation), and how this will affect your dependents. It's important to do this as it will kick you into action, moving these matters up your list of priorities and leading you to the second step: taking responsibility for it.

You now know what the worst possible outcome is, so there's no excuse. Be responsible and head straight to step three: work hard to

---

1 Author of 'How to Win Friends and Influence People'.

improve it. Make an appointment to see a solicitor today, or pick up a will kit at the post office and fill it in. Ring an insurance agent (or at least ring your superannuation fund) and select an appropriate amount of life insurance.

It's simply a matter of taking action.

Another example

Let's say your top two priorities involve non-deductible debt—in this case a home loan and several out-of-control credit cards—and there's no budget in place.

Step one: think of the worst possible outcome. You may go broke, be forced to sell your house or never be able to retire (and because you don't have a budget in place, you won't be able to establish the reasons why).

Step two: stop the excuses and take responsibility for it. Drag yourself away from the TV for a few nights, download a budget template from the internet and draw up a budget.

Step three: start working hard on improving the situation. Look at consolidating the credit cards into your home loan at a much lower interest rate, and then cut those credit cards up (except possibly for an emergency card). Make the necessary spending cuts to live within your budget and know precisely when (in years) your home loan will finally be repaid.

And yet another example

Let's say your top two priorities involve four superannuation fund balances across four different commercial funds, you have no idea what their performance is like or how much you're being charged in fees, and you have no other investments.

Step one: think of the worst possible outcome. You're wasting money—your money—real money that you may have been able to access and of course spend on retirement, or leave to your dependents should the worst happen. Ignoring this is simply reducing your ability to retire, and the quality of life you'll have when you eventually do.

Step two: take responsibility. It's entirely your fault (and there's no point blaming old employers).

Step three: see an advisor or review the funds yourself and put them in order (for example, by consolidating them in a self-managed fund).

If your fund balance is sufficient, you can even think about borrowing against it to make another investment, bringing your retirement prospects even closer (more about that later).

Once you've addressed the top two priorities we move onto the next two priorities, and so on.

So what happens now?

The rest of this book is full of case studies that address every single point I've made here (and that the index contains).

Let me show you precisely how you can embark on removing the financial distractions from your life.

PART THREE

THE LIVES OF OTHERS

CHAPTER ONE

WHY WE WORK

There are a lot of socially acceptable answers I can give you when it comes to the question of why we work. The reality for most of us, though, is that we work to survive. And most of us are in precisely the same boat, asking the same types of questions when it comes to why it is we work and what it is we're trying to achieve (and in that respect, this chapter really sets the tone for the rest of this book).

So let's start coming to grips with this question.

Income often sets our standard of living. Can you remember your first job and how little you earned? At the time, I'll bet you thought it was a small fortune. You may have been able to spend a little on just plain having fun, and even save a little for your first car or your first trip overseas. Thinking about it today, though, I'll also bet you wonder how anyone could have possibly survived on such a paltry sum.

As we earn more we usually spend more (unless you're extremely disciplined), and this can often dictate why, how, and where we work. So spending is really not only about survival, but is also often about choice, particularly when it comes to discretionary spending.

No matter what our position is, it's always within our power to do something about our circumstances. We can work harder and longer, or we can pursue better-paid (although usually more stressful) jobs and careers to meet our level of spending. Quite often, though, this is simply a false pursuit, as our spending continues to increase with the larger income.

Rather than chasing a bigger income, more stress and significantly more financial distraction, could it be that we merely need to view things a little differently, to the point where the income we receive from the labour we sell is *not* the critical decision when it comes to *why* we do it?

Work and money, and the massive financial distraction these two things represent, is where we'll begin.

Work and money

Many people believe that the way ahead, both financially and from the perspective of status, is forged by climbing the promotional ladder. To an extent this is true, but there are easier (and smarter) alternatives.

Clearly, moving up the organisational hierarchy provides both financial benefits as well as status, but so does building a terrific personal investment portfolio. In fact, some people argue that this is a much smarter way to progress, as it leads to several crucial things: passive income, a greater net worth, and greater choices when it comes to whether you have to work for a salary or not.

I've seen too many executives work hard for their money, pay their taxes, and then pay themselves last. They simply don't have time to manage their investments, and so are unaware of the possibilities. Most of the time, they'll either outsource their investment choices to advisers, with all the corresponding commissions and results, or they'll not participate at all and rely on their salaries. The problem at this stage is that eventually they'll stop working, and if they haven't educated themselves by actively participating in the investment choices being made on their behalf, then their retirement income and therefore their lifestyles may be significantly affected.

But maybe there's a smarter choice.

By spending more time focusing on personal investments early on in life, you can actually rid yourself of the need for climbing that promotional ladder to make more money, which places promotional advancement solely in the category of personal challenge and development. Putting it simply, personal success is more likely if your reason for advancement isn't being driven by your finances or perceived status.

There are other advantages from having a solid investment portfolio. Having a good overall financial position reduces work stress and pressure, which often leads to improved performance at work, clarity of thought, and significantly improved relationships. If you're constantly worrying about the next promotion, pay rise, or bonus, you won't be performing at your best. When you know that your investment portfolio growth is averaging 8% per annum, though, worrying about whether your bonus is $5,000 or $25,000 hardly matters, especially given you'll have to pay tax on it anyway!

Getting your investment portfolio in order also allows more time for socialising and improving yourself in other areas. This naturally tends to improve your lifestyle and work/life balance making you better at work as a direct result, which can only enhance your promotional prospects even further.

The fact is that you can have the best car in the car park not because you have the most senior role, but because you've got one of the best investment portfolios.

There's many a humble factory worker or office secretary in a better financial position than their managers. In fact, I see it all the time. And they're most often the quiet ones, astute enough to have bought a portfolio of shares or a property when they were young, then going on to buy another and another as their equity and cash flow improved.

In a way, your life can become a vortex that either drives you to work harder at work or spins you off to financial independence and a much better, more rounded approach to life.

So how do we get there?

Ideally, the first step is to start young, but if you've missed that boat, then starting anytime is still a positive, even if you're in your fifties. It's really never too late to start focussing on building an enviable retirement strategy that will put you on the path to being able to make choices.

If you have children, then start educating them now so they start investing early. It really does make a world of difference in their lives, even more so than any mega-dollar educational head-start you may give them.

Okay, so if the first step is starting young, or just starting, then what's the next step? Two words: cash flow.

Cash flow

To be honest, most people tune out at this point, and that's because I always start this topic with a discussion about budgeting. Talking about budgeting has to be about the most boring, unattractive, uninteresting and mundane way to spend an evening. (And if you don't believe me—and remember, this is coming from an accountant—sit down and do one tonight.) The problem is that they're essential if you want to create a future passive income stream.

So how do we budget?

Try an internet search using the key words 'free budget templates'. At last count, there were nearly 42 million results you could select from.

In reality, though, there's nothing hard about doing a budget, and the way I often encourage my clients to start is by either downloading the data from their credit card and bank statements for the past 12 months, or when a data download isn't possible, to manually record this information on a simple spreadsheet. The point is, by doing this for a 12-month period, we can effectively measure our spending habits (though sometimes I'm sure we'd rather not know).

The next step is to classify the data by putting it into different columns like 'motor vehicle', 'food', 'entertainment', 'alcohol', 'travel', 'utility bills', 'phones', 'rent', 'mortgage', 'insurance', 'repairs', 'household items', 'gifts', 'medical', 'family', 'education', 'clothing', etc. The list can be as long or short as you want it to be.

When you know where the money has gone, you can start to manage future expenditure more effectively, and for the simple reason that you can't manage what you haven't measured.

So how do you start managing your spending? You start by simply making budget choices. For example, by stopping some expenses and controlling others, and by reviewing and re-negotiating your outlays (getting quotes), all with the aim of creating a surplus you can invest. That investment, no matter how small, creates more income that starts to accumulate (Einstein's eighth wonder of the world: compound interest!), with the aim of creating more income over the coming years.

It really doesn't matter how small or large the surplus is. The outcome is always the same whenever we accumulate savings and investments and increase personal income: it improves our ability to make choices.

For example, maybe someone close to you needs critical care. Being able to make choices means you can seriously consider retiring earlier so you can help. Or maybe you want to travel or volunteer your life abroad. Having choices enables you to do it.

Having enough and not *needing* to work is the primary motivation I'm trying to instil. Choice is sometimes a tough word, but we nearly always have choices. Making a start is a choice. Reading this book is a choice. So make the choice.

Survival

If you're in financial survival mode or suffering cash flow deficits out of necessity (for example, because you're raising a family on one income, trying to meet hefty school fees, or facing ongoing medical expenses), then no matter how you look at, if you're still working, even part time, you still have a surplus (one you have usually forgotten about), because some of your wage goes to superannuation.

So stay positive and treat your surplus superannuation seriously. Throughout this book I'll show you superannuation strategies and 'passage of time solutions' that work on any income level, even when you're in a budget deficit. These strategies are critical to understanding and addressing the financial distractions that are inevitably linked with why we work.

To put all this into some context though, I want to close out this early chapter with an example of hope.

Hope

I have a favourite saying:
'*Happiness lies within the absence of want.*'

Ironically, it was a difficult divorce that first helped me on my journey to achieve that, allowing me finally to be able to let go of material things, but the wake-up call can come anytime and from anywhere, whether it's a bankruptcy, fire, stock market crash, flood, theft, or even a serious illness. As unpleasant as they appear, these events can all prove to be positives when it comes to learning about the benefits of not being bound by financial distraction.

For me, with a career in finance and having witnessed great unhappiness springing from wealth and spending, particularly during the credit crisis and the market crashes of 2008, I like to share the following story with clients who have suffered the most (often whether they like it or not) as a way of bringing things into perspective:

> *It can cost only $5.00 to entertain family or guests to a memorable day out. In Australia, we're blessed with beautiful beaches, parks and lakes. So let's say we pick a day to go to the beach. On this day, we choose not to park in a council car park, making the car parking free for the day. Let's say we also choose to keep lunch simple: around $2.00 for a simple crusty loaf, and maybe $3.00 for a packet of cheese (and with water brought from home, the drinks are as good as free).*
>
> *Children won't care if they're on a beach in Hawaii or one closer to home, and if your guests do, then that's their problem (give them this book).*
>
> *Have a swim. Try building a sand castle or digging a hole for the kids to jump into (the adults too). Just don't forget to take a camera!*
>
> *What do you think will be the more memorable event for your children or guests? Yet another affair at a restaurant or your home, or the day you showed them all that life is for living and entertained them on a beach for the day?*

Examples of really living are all around us. It costs absolutely nothing to sit on a park bench and talk to everyone who passes by that day. It costs equally as much simply to sit in quiet solitude, watching a tide come in.

Put life into perspective.

CHAPTER TWO

WORK/LIFE BALANCE

One of the best pieces of advice I have ever received came to me as I was first starting off in accounting and finance, and just one month before the birth of my first beautiful child.

Accounting and finance is a very demanding and time-intensive profession that can at times be mentally exhausting. The advice was relatively simple (if not a little difficult to achieve at times, though I was yet to experience that): make time for your children while they're still young, because once they've matured and established their own identities and no longer have much time left over for you, that moment has gone forever.

Making your children a priority is not the only point I'm going to make in this chapter. That's just the most obvious priority to highlight. Equally important priorities include making time for your spouse, time for your hobbies, time for friendships, sport, travel, and even rest and sleep.

All these considerations are part of maintaining a work/life balance, and the amount of guilt and dissatisfaction I see in clients who aren't getting this balance right makes for a tremendous distraction generally, not to mention being financially distracting, because they're often making the wrong decisions when it comes to getting this balance right.

Coming back to that early advice I received (which I don't claim for a minute to have gotten totally right), I very much took it to heart. So I'd often start at stupidly early times, well before dawn, so I could walk out the door at 5:00 PM and be able have a quick play, share dinner, and do baths with them.

No matter what your work/life balance is, the only way to achieve any balance at all is to be absolutely rigid with your time management and priority setting. Some people are naturally extremely good at this, and others are absolutely hopeless at it (and should seriously consider some time-management courses and take responsibility for improving this part of their lives).

Wherever you sit on this scale, you can always improve and so remove the distractions that come from an ineffective use of time and a poor work/life balance.

Before we examine the case study for this chapter, I'd like to briefly talk about a fairly famous play called *Death of a Salesman* by the playwright Arthur Miller. Specifically, I want to talk about the play's main character, Willy Loman (and if you've never seen, read, or even heard about this play, then do yourself a favour and look it up).

One of the play's key themes ran along these lines: you work a lifetime to pay off a house until you finally own it, only by then there's nobody left at home to live in it. Ironically, the final payment on Willy Loman's house was made after Willy, the man who'd worked so hard all his life to pay for it, had died.

And with that sobering thought in mind, let's look at our first example:

> *A skilled industrial worker works long hours to demonstrate his loyalty and diligence to his firm. In the process, he gives up a much beloved sport so he can work on Saturdays and do*

even longer hours during the week, all of which tires him out to the point that he can only actually take a short break on his Sundays (and even then he sometimes finds himself back at work if there's a backlog).

What our worker is angling for is a partnership in the business, and he's already started to take emotional ownership of the workplace as if the partnership is a forgone conclusion (when it's actually anything but). This situation persists for many years and the owners do nothing to change it, because they're effectively already getting a partner without having to meet the cost of one.

Now consider a nightmare scenario unfolds: the owner's son decides he wants to work in the business and overnight our worker's ranking abruptly drops. Follow this up with an industry downturn with the available work plummeting to minimum hours and no certainty of anymore ongoing, and who's more likely to be retrenched first?

The reality now is, though, that there's no business for him to buy into (which would be crazy to do, even if he could), not to mention the fact that the goal posts have been moved. Our worker's previous conscientious effort has not only gone unrewarded, but has been for nothing, and he's now underemployed and probably heading for retrenchment.

It's a bad situation to be in. So let's look at this example in a little more detail.

It's good to work hard and please the boss (especially if you're one of my employees!), but bosses that push their workers too hard or don't understand the importance of work/life balance are the exact type of employer you should avoid. They don't have your best interests at heart, and as we saw in this example, the owner of the business was more than happy to take whatever his employee was prepared to give and when the crunch came, showed a propensity to give little to nothing in return.

There will always be times when we need to make sacrifices when it comes to work, but only under certain circumstances, when it's really necessary.

At the time of writing this chapter, economic uncertainty was on the rise and an increasing risk of retrenchment and unemployment always suggests it's a good idea to start making sacrifices so that, if it comes to it, you're the last person out the door (and not the first). This eventually changes, of course, and as demand for employees rises, you start to get your work/life balance back into kilter.

The key point of the example I've provided in this chapter, though, is to measure your time and your sacrifices against a realistic probability of reward, and not to just hope for the best. When you're making sacrifices for work, always make sure there's good (and realistic) cause to do so.

A major bugbear of mine (and something I've definitely been guilty of in the past) concerns the reasons why we push ourselves to work longer and harder when we're young, only so we can retire earlier. By the time we retire, we're older and less physically able to do things we enjoy, not to mention having significantly less time to spend with the people we love (our children and parents).

Isn't it more sensible to work a little less hard and retire later in life, so we can take time to enjoy life right now, while we're at the peak of our physical capabilities and still surrounded by our loved ones? Why run the risk of a major health issue well before we're actually due to retire, and so risk not being able to do the things we love later on in life anyway?

Speaking personally, it just doesn't make sense.

Really, though, staying active is the key to being both attractive (and by 'attractive' I effectively mean attracting work opportunities, attracting people when you're networking, and attracting employers) and to getting your work/life balance right, and one of my favourite words is 'participate'.

Get active in life, in your sporting club, your spiritual life, hobbies and schools. Be exciting to be around and watch the right financial opportunities come your way.

SUMMING IT ALL UP

Try to have a 'board of directors' for your life. These are people whose opinion you value and who'll give you honest replies when you run your work/life balance issues past them.

Always address your work/life balance issues and be at peace with your choices when they're the right choices made for the right reasons, because by doing so, you can finally bring these work/life balance distractions to an end.

CHAPTER THREE

THE COST OF CHILDREN

What a financial distraction raising children can be! And having said this, I now want to clarify: having children is by far and away the greatest thing that has ever happened in my life, and financial considerations never figured.

Going from two wages to one and/or having to meet childcare costs and all the additional expenses of feeding, medicating, and clothing a child, all bring significant financial distraction that needs to be addressed and put into context if we want to avoid spoiling what should be the wonderful experience of nurturing and raising your family.

When I started thinking about writing this chapter, I pretty quickly realised it needed to be broken up into age groups. Two generations ago, families were traditionally started while the parents were in their early twenties, which meant by the time the parents had reached their early to mid-forties, the children would have moved out or started contributing to the household. Back then, you would have had two decades to save for retirement without the costs of raising children.

Nowadays, families are being started much later, and more often than not when the parents are in their mid-thirties, and even up until their early forties. To add to the equation, children tend to be moving out later and contributing a great deal less (or even nothing at all), so you now have very little time at all to financially 'recover' for retirement.

In a lot of cases, parents haven't been saving much (if at all) prior to starting their family, because they've been off seeing the world and generally enjoying being young and childless.

I'll call these two different groups 'early bloomers' and 'late bloomers'.

One of the saving graces for late bloomers is the early start they made to their superannuation, which has been accumulating for both parents (although most don't take this investment all that seriously, although they should, especially with such a small window of time left to prepare for retirement).

Late bloomers should also be considering a range of tax-effective, negatively-geared investments while they still have some surplus income (there should be surpluses at some point, as incomes at this time of life are usually higher).

Early bloomers face an entirely different scenario. More often than not, one spouse has very little superannuation because they stopped work very early to raise the children, and the working spouse will continue to add to superannuation but will rarely have any other investments because the wages are generally smaller at the start of a career (and only tend to increase as we grow older).

Then we have the 'in-betweeners' (this group falls somewhere between the early and the late bloomers) and the 'mixed-bloomers' (partnerships comprising an early *and* a late bloomer), both of which require a hybrid of the early and late bloomer investment approaches.

I don't go into much detail in this chapter when it comes to in-betweeners and mixed-bloomers, but by understanding the early and late bloomers you'll have the tools you need to create your own strategy hybrids, or be able to sit down with a professional who can work through one with you.

The critical point here is that no matter what your age, and no matter how much you actually outlay (even if it's only relatively minor), you need to invest.

Investment gives us life choices (choices we wouldn't otherwise have if we didn't have the additional assets investment provides) and anything that will compound and grow will do the trick.

Early bloomers

Don and Donna met in their teen years, married young, and had three children by the time they were both 25. Donna has no superannuation. Don has $25,000 in superannuation and earns $45,000 a year. Donna plans to return to part-time work when her youngest child is in grade two, and full-time work when all three are in secondary school (but this is still some time away).

Just after they got married, Don and Donna bought a home for $250,000, which is now worth $350,000, so they've built up some good equity. With the mortgage at a manageable $180,000, their 'cost of living under a roof' has been contained.

This is a very different scenario to a late bloomer and requires an altogether different focus. Non-deductible debt (like a housing loan or credit card debt) is bad debt and any spare income should be used to repay it. The problem the early bloomer faces is that there won't be much of that for a while.

Surplus income is the obvious problem for the early bloomer, and as the cost of living is about to increase and incomes decrease (to one wage), it's time to change our spending habits and do a budget. Government (tax-free) allowances for families should be applied for, and Donna should possibly be considering doing some causal work, as well.

Given there will be little or no surplus income (in fact, the early bloomers may even be spending more than they're making at this stage), negatively-geared investments are pointless. At this point, neutrally-geared investment strategies can be considered, such as borrowing to buy blue-chip, high-dividend yielding stocks that will pay enough of a dividend to cover the interest expense. An investment like this doesn't impact annual cash flow, and potentially even adds to it as inflation increases the dividend yield over time, exceeding the interest expense.

Having a small superannuation base of $25,000 that will increase with contributions and earnings is not the major asset in this example, the family home is, and superannuation should not become their focus until the children grow up, because they'll have time to add to their superannuation balances later on. That said, reviewing, consolidating, and minimising the fees they pay on those funds is still something they need to take very seriously. It's still an asset and it will become a major focus once the children are old enough (and the childrearing expenses have diminished). At this stage, though, they don't need to consider making extra contributions to their superannuation for quite a few years yet.

Late bloomers

Peter and Mary have been living the dream. Travelling to Europe and America with their professions, they've taken long holidays, spent up on fancy cars, shoes, clothes, whatever they've really wanted. It really has been a great life for them both. But they're both in their late thirties now and ready to settle down and start a family.

> *The years of living the dream have left them with nothing but $50,000 each in superannuation, no other assets, and a couple of ugly credit card debts totalling $20,000. Peter earns well at $100,000 a year and so did Mary, but they've decided it will be of more benefit to their new family if Mary stops work and stays at home to raise the three children they plan to have.*

This scenario's focus really is on debt. We have to get back to square one before we can grow and move on. The credit card debts should be consolidated and moved into a lower interest alternative, or even better into an interest-free loan from family (future grandparents can become quite generous at this point in time). We also have to put together a budget.

The cost of living for our late bloomer couple is about to increase and their incomes decrease, so it's high time to start changing spending habits, and a budget will help them monitor and measure their outlays.

Just as in our early bloomer example, government (tax-free) allowances for families should be investigated and applied for, and Mary should also be considering a little causal work.

Unfortunately, buying a home is out of the question for quite some time. The upside is that renting is cheaper than buying, and once their debts are repaid they can start to accumulate savings in the form of cash and possibly some blue-chip dividend-yielding shares. After a while, they can consider buying a rental/investment property (in Peter's name only), and take advantage of a little negative gearing.

To be very clear, there's no magic pill here. By being sensible and actually making a start, over time Peter's wage will increase and Mary will return to work, and the choice about whether to buy a family home will eventually be available to them. The point is that if they do nothing, then nothing will compound into nothing. They simply *must* make a start.

Unlike our early bloomer example, their combined superannuation base of $100,000 is their only asset, so reviewing, consolidating and reducing fess on the funds is something to take even more seriously. In fact, because they'll not be able to significantly add to it after their child-rearing years, they may also consider additional contributions to their superannuation to increase the fund balance early, and so reduce the need for top-ups later on in their working lives.

Single parents

What about single parents? While I don't specifically consider single parents in this chapter, my chapter on Divorce has plenty of solid tips and information that's more directly relevant to a single parent's unique circumstances, and will enable you to use this chapter as a framework.

Is it better to buy them a home than an education?

I've introduced this final thought as a bit of a throw-away topic to challenge our thinking. That said, it's a thought that, depending on your circumstances, may be well worth considering.

With the cost of putting a child through private schooling nearing $200,000 or more (not allowing for the income we're foregoing if we'd otherwise invested this amount), are we actually better off to save this money on their behalf, and use it to provide a kick-start into a property for them later on in life?

The sacrifices a family needs to make to afford private schooling can often be immense, with both spouses working and the family's debts either remaining outstanding or even mounting (and just think about the financial distraction involved with this situation).

But is the government school system really that bad?

Most teachers I've met are clever people, and all too often students are letting themselves down through inattention or a failure to apply themselves to their studies. So aren't we better off finding schools (or mentors) that do a better job, and then supporting them by teaching our children *how* to learn from the resources put before them instead of needing to be intensively taught?

Everyone's circumstances differ, of course, but you have to wonder whether it's actually better to teach our children how to educate themselves, rather than effectively delegating that task.

All this said, every child is different and needs differ, and I personally think private education can offer a tremendous start for children who need it.

CHAPTER FOUR

THE THREE PILLARS

Now it's time to tie the first three chapters into the passage of time and ultimately retirement planning, which can probably best be described as an all-consuming, life-time financial distraction!

In the main, we work to survive.

To retire, though, we need to stop work and *still* be able to survive. And to do that we need to accumulate sufficient assets while we're working, and it's probably a rare moment when we're not thinking about precisely that end game (unless it's all become too hard and you're ignoring it, which is a much worse place to be).

One useful rule of thumb to use when determining how much you need at retirement is to apply a multiplier of your desired income to determine the lump sum you're going to need. It's a simplistic method and we'll get into various other multipliers for men, women and particular age groups a little later on.

Let's look at some examples.

> *Let's say you're a 55 year-old man. You'll need assets totalling 17 times your desired income stream. Say you require $40,000 per annum (let's say without rent or mortgage costs). You'll need assets totalling approximately $680,000. This may or may not include the family home, depending on your desired outcome,*

but you should allow for extra income to pay rent. There's nothing wrong with using the family home (in my mind, only don't tell my kids), but most parents want to leave something for their children, or have some kind of final financial back-up for added security.

Let's say you're a 55 year-old woman. Based on the life expectancy averages, you're going to live longer, and you'll need assets totalling approximately 18 times your desired income stream ($720,000) for the same outcome.

If you're a couple both aged 55 and you require a joint income of $60,000 ($30,000 each), then in this case we'd take 75% to allow for the shared costs of the two lump sum amounts (which is $510,000 in the case of the man and $540,000 in the case of the woman) and come up with a combined balance of $1,050,000, which is not technically correct, as the wife will live another two years, but as a rule of thumb it's certainly close enough.

Remember, this is only a rule of thumb calculation and there are many other considerations you need to take into account when doing a formal plan for retirement. For example, acceptable levels of risk, market volatilities, types of investments, inherent or other health issues, other dependents (handicapped children, siblings, etc), possible future inheritances to be received, or downsizing the family home. As you can see, the list of considerations can be a long one.

The Lump Sum Needed for Men Aged:

55 = 17 times the desired income stream

60 = 15 times the desired income stream

65 = 13 times the desired income stream

The Lump Sum Needed for Women Aged:
55 = 18 times the desired income stream
60 = 17 times the desired income stream
65 = 15 times the desired income stream

The problem with the rule of thumb, and accumulating the lump sum required, is that people often don't understand how this works in terms of the passage of time, or how they can use their existing assets to achieve it (and if you think you're in this boat, then go back to Using Positives at the start of the book and re-read the case study for the passage of time).

Let's look at another example.

> *You're 38 years old with a fluctuating mortgage, your youngest child hasn't started primary school yet, and your stay-at-home parent hasn't returned to work yet.*

How do we show this couple how their nest egg will accumulate into a retirement pool?

The Three Pillars is a tool I created a long time ago, but still use almost daily with my clients to help them understand their financial priorities within the context of passing time.

So what are the Three Pillars?

Pillar 1 – Tax-Effective Investing
Pillar 2 – Your Own Home
Pillar 3 – Superannuation

The journey through the Three Pillars starts with some form of investing and anything will do (whether it's shares, bonds, or an investment property), along with using the tax system to assist with reaching the point where you're able to buy your own home, until ultimately we end up with superannuation as we approach our retirement years.

While I call them the Three Pillars, the order you approach them in often varies. For example, you usually start contributing to superannuation as soon as you start work, but we only really consider superannuation to be a priority when we're older (usually over fifty).

Similarly, we usually invest in shares (potentially via some tax-effective and protected margin lending) as a way of accumulating sufficient assets to buy a family home, then turn our attention towards reducing non-deductible debt before considering tax-effective investing again.

Let's start with Pillar 1, which is really where our focus should begin.

Pillar 1 – Tax-Effective Investing

Most people will start tax-effective investing through savings or shares (which in most cases is what we recommend), as there isn't sufficient equity to buy property just yet.

Contrary to common belief, savings can be tax-effective. For example, if a high income earner in a couple or a family places their savings in the name of a partner or spouse earning a lower (or no) income, this can effectively reduce or even eliminate the tax on any interest earned.

At the time of writing, the yield on shares is nearly the same as interest rates on borrowings, so the holding costs are close enough to neutral. Shares are still considered to be tax-effective, though, as most dividends have a franking (imputation) credit, which is a credit for tax already paid by the company (and guess what, you get that, too, which sounds pretty tax-effective if you ask me).

Say we scrape together $5,000 and borrow (margin lend) another $5,000 and buy shares worth $10,000. Let's say we can add another $500 per month to this together with another $500 in borrowings.

The interest bill on every $10,000 investment ($5,000 equity + $5,000 borrowed at 8%) will be $400 per year, and the dividends from the shares will be $600 (including the franking credits on $10,000), so we're actually cash flow positive to the tune of $200 a year, while we're also hoping for an average annual growth in our shares' value of around 8% or $800 compounding.

This is usually a very effective form of Pillar 1 savings using leverage. The problem is timing, and a five-year outlook for shares is advisable, as dips can take a while to recover from. The best time to start investing is during a market dip, or if you've been caught out by a dip yourself, then think about increasing your contributions or exposure if possible, effectively meaning we're 'dollar cost averaging' by buying more shares while the price is low (basically decreasing the average cost of each share), which brings down our initial entry point (cost) while we're still receiving dividends.

It's not all bad in a dip!

We then use the accumulated Pillar 1 funds to feed into Pillar 2 and buying your own home. Alternatively, if you're not quite in that position yet, we may consider an investment property, either on your own or in partnership with others.

Let's consider an example.

Loan for a house/unit	$400,000
Interest payable at 6%	($24,000)
Rates, repairs, body corporate, etc	($2,500)
Rent received	$19,500
For a cash flow loss	**($7,000)**

Now take into account the taxation considerations:

Non-cash chattel depreciation	($1,500)
Non-cash building depreciation at 2.5%	($7,500)
For a tax loss	($16,000)
Tax refund on the tax loss (at 34%)	$5,440
Total cash flow loss	**($1,560)**

In this example we're looking at a tax rate of 34%. But the tax saving rises to $7,440 for a tax payer in the top tax bracket (financial year 2013), to a $440 cash flow gain!

Once again, we're facing a minor cash flow loss at worst, and if we consider even a conservative capital growth rate of 5%, this equates to $20,000 per annum compounding on a property already worth $400,000.

A great strategy when buying an investment property with limited capital is to go into the purchase with friends or family, buy a dump and spend your weekends doing the place up, increasing both the rental income return and the capital value.

Ultimately, any Pillar 1 investment pathway, whether it be shares, property, cash, or other investments I haven't mentioned here, should ultimately lead us to Pillar 2, where that Pillar 1 equity can be used to purchase our own home.

Pillar 2 – Your Own Home

Some while ago, in my accounting practice's regular newsletter, I challenged my clients on the wisdom of owning a home to live in (Pillar 2), suggesting that a better option may involve investing in rental property, while living in a rental property themselves.

Regardless to say, it was probably one of the most controversial newsletters I have ever published, judging from the responses we received, which were often quite passionate and overwhelmingly in favour of home ownership.

For the record, I own my home and think everyone should (Pillar 2), and for reasons that often don't necessarily stack up numerically, which I'll talk about next.

So here are the main points for and against buying your own home.

To buy a home, or rent and invest instead?

Stock standard advice when it comes to personal finances has generally always involved buying a property to live in. But have we now reached a pricing point where renting is becoming the better option? Is buying a home for half a million dollars or more (plus stamp duty and other costs and charges) financially realistic anymore?

Arguments in favour of this notion include the fact that you avoid a significant debt burden (stress), rent is cheaper than paying interest (and you avoid the risk of rising interest rates), you can afford to rent a better place than you can afford to buy that's closer to your work with reduced travel costs and travel times (quality of life), and you avoid having to perform or pay for ongoing repairs and maintenance.

Arguments against this notion are that rent money is dead money, you don't benefit from the property's capital growth, there's a measure of insecurity when it comes to rent increases and how long you will actually be able to stay in the property, you enjoy no feeling of ownership, and you forgo the opportunity to make capital improvements.

The arguments against can be partly addressed by owning your own rental property or other investments (shares, etc) and so gain capital growth that way. Asking for a longer lease (quite common overseas) will offer lease security and help to manage potential rent increases (and why not ask for a two, three or even a five-year lease with CPI increases; they work for both the tenant and the landlord and are the norm with commercial real estate).

Consider the following case.

> *You buy a cheaper property in an area where you'd like to retire when you're older (at the beach or in the country), or simply as an investment in a growth area, then rent it out while continuing to live or rent in an area where you want to be (close to work/city/schools) prior to retiring, saving and further investing the difference in even more property or shares (my favourite) or even safely invested superannuation (Pillar 3) when you're close to retirement.*

Who's to say who's right or who's wrong with these scenarios?

The big problem with this logic, though, is that Australians generally have an inability to save and a propensity to spend, yet they're able to repay their mortgages quickly. So why do Australians pay off loans relatively fast, when a big chunk of the world looks at housing debt as just debt, and pays it off over a longer period? Why the rush? Why don't we make interest-only repayments or have longer payback periods (25 years or more) and invest or save elsewhere (or even have a better quality of life)? I haven't really been able to answer this question. I believe it's cultural, and so we pay the banks back as quickly as we can, making sacrifices along the way to do it.

In reality, I think most of us find saving quite difficult and paying off a mortgage becomes a form of forced saving, which is why owning your home forms the basis for Pillar 2 (and even for an accountant with a doctorate, the reasoning is still much the same).

Pillar 3 – Superannuation

Tax-effective investment doesn't get any better than when we're making pre-tax contributions to superannuation. I go into the effectiveness of superannuation, including self-managed superannuation and borrowing against your superannuation, in some detail later on in my chapters on Divorce and Farming with Superannuation.

Superannuation contributions are taxed at a low 15%. Compare this to the 34% tax rate most taxpayers face, and for every $100 you salary sacrifice into superannuation, you have an immediate saving of $19.00 in tax.[2]

Simply by putting money into superannuation you have made an immediate 19% return on your pre-tax money (or the equivalent at the time of writing of around four years of term deposit interest).

In this chapter, though, I'm going to talk about superannuation in the context of the Three Pillars and the transition to retirement.

Transition to Retirement

If you're currently aged 55, still working and haven't considered a Transition to Retirement strategy, then you need to review your situation as soon as possible. In most cases, if you're sixty and not already using a Transition to Retirement strategy, you're currently experiencing some serious and very unnecessary pain.

So what is Transition to Retirement?

Transition to Retirement refers to the ability to use your existing superannuation funds to begin a Transition to Retirement Pension (TRP), using those pension payments to fund tax-effective saving

---

2 The tax saving rises to $31.50 for a tax payer in the top tax bracket for 2013.

strategies, such as additional voluntary superannuation contributions from salary sacrifice (for which you can receive a tax deduction).

Let's look at a brief example.

> *You've reached sixty and withdraw $12,000 from your superannuation fund tax free (you can withdraw up to a maximum of 10% of your superannuation fund balance each year, whereas the minimum amounts you need to withdraw each year are age dependent) and salary sacrifice $12,000 back into your superannuation fund.*
>
> *This transaction saves you $2,280 in tax alone when you're on the average tax rate of 34% (given you only pay 15% on the salary-sacrificed contribution, a net return of 19%).*

Let me repeat that (and bold it for some added oomph): **an immediate return of 19%.**

And it gets even better.

Transferring your superannuation funds from the 'accumulation' phase to the Transition to Retirement 'pension' phase provides immediate tax savings on the income your superannuation fund assets earn. Income earned on assets invested in the 'accumulation' phase is taxed at 10% to 15%, while income earned on assets invested in the 'pension' phase is not taxed at all.

This is often overlooked, but let me show you how the savings work in practice.

> *You've managed to accumulate $300,000 in superannuation at the age of sixty. This $300,000 earns a long-term average of 8%, or $24,000 per year, which is taxed at 15% ($3,600). Of course, you never see this tax bill, as the superannuation fund pays it for you, deducting it from your member account earnings.*

In the two stages of this example, if you salary sacrificed $12,000 per year and funded that by starting a transition to retirement pension, you'll save $2,280 in tax (which is the difference between the 34% ($4,080) tax rate the average taxpayer pays and the 15% ($1,800) superannuation rate).

As the lump sum funds the transition to the 'pension' phase, you're paying no tax at all and so saving an additional average of $3,600, representing a total saving of $5,880 ($2,280 plus the $3,600 you'd otherwise have been paying).

Too good to be true? It's a tax-effective reality! So give yourself a swift kick if you're sixty years old and not already doing this right now!

As the general advice warning at the start of the book reminds us, circumstances differ and other issues, for example anti-detriment or untaxed funds, may need to be considered, so always get advice based on your personal circumstances.

The Three Pillars and the passage of time

Generally speaking, the Three Pillars deal with the passage of time in the following ways:

PILLAR 1:

- Focus on tax-effective investments and savings from the moment you enter the workforce.
- Think about starting the savings initially with a share portfolio (for example by moving into Exchange Traded Funds (ETF), which I'll talk about later on in the book) and speed the process by re-investing the dividends for growth instead of cash.
- Accumulate the savings for a deposit on a rental property or other investments.

PILLAR 2:

- Home ownership. Aim to commence this phase around marrying age (say mid-twenties to thirties), depending on when or if this happens to you, of course. At this point we look at moving all of Pillar 1 into Pillar 2 (your home).

PILLAR 3:

- Superannuation. This really should always be the focus. Although you should always treat your superannuation seriously even when you're young, this pillar becomes a major focus once you've reached fifty.

SUMMING IT ALL UP

Think about using your Pillar 1 investments to fund the transition to Pillar 2 (your own home). Once achieving Pillar 2 that equity also accumulates, and can be used for some tax-effective re-investment (via Pillar 1-type investments) right up to the age of fifty, when Pillar 3 (superannuation) becomes a priority.

Keep the Three Pillars in mind and modify them as required when you're planning for retirement, and the stages to pass through on that journey will become a lot clearer. Alternatively, sit down with a financial planner who can clarify the passage of time for you and provide a road map for you to follow, and remove this all-consuming financial distraction once and for all!

CHAPTER FIVE

TAX JEALOUSIES

This book may well be fully tax deductible! (For most of you, anyway, under the label of 'tax advice' on your tax return. Speak to your accountant to clarify details if you need to.)

As a seasoned tax accountant, I often come across what I call 'tax-jealousy'.

I can hear you asking the next obvious question already …

Excuse the medical puns in this chapter. Being a doctor and all, this could get a little tongue in cheek (how else does one make a chapter on tax interesting?), so let me describe the common ailment of 'tax jealousy' with a 'pressing' example.

Tax jealousy refers to the way a person feels (and usually a PAYG employee) when they look at their payslip and the amount of tax they're paying, and they compare it to a self-employed or negatively-geared investor's tax returns. That feeling (naturally) is one of resentment about the fact they're paying more.

Thankfully, as a practicing doctor (of tax-effective investing), I have a cure for this affliction. Tax-jealousy can be treated with daily doses of rebuttal from someone like me. We know your financial position, how much you can borrow, and how easily you too can join the ranks of healthy investors enjoying significant tax-effective investment growth over time.

Anyone aspiring to be in peak financial shape is already using equity in his or her property, cash in the bank, or even surplus income to support an investment loan. Way too many people are suprised to find there's almost always an income surplus when your spending is being held to account through budgeting. But the reality is that soon enough, you too can be tripping along the road to tax recovery along with all the others!

There's a caveat, though.

You don't want to catch a bout of unnecessary RISK along the way. No one can be immune to risk, but the self-employed and the negatively-geared investor have already received their booster shots (though I'll be focussing on the negatively-geared investor, because not everyone wants to be self-employed). Negative gearing means making an investment loss on your other sources of income (and getting a tax refund) in exchange for longer-term capital gains from a growth asset.

The risks here are that the gains may not be made, or the capital may be partially or completely lost.

Let's look at an example.

> *You've just borrowed $100,000 to invest in shares at an average interest rate of 8%, costing you $8,000 per year. Let's say the dividend income from the shares is 4% (returning $4,000 per year) and also comes with a 1% dividend franking imputation credit of $1,000 that you don't see in cash but will see in your tax return.*
>
> *The negative gearing stems from the net loss of $3,000, which is then neatly offset against your taxable income, meaning tax refunds at your marginal tax rate (it's pretty simple stuff and it's the same for property as well).*

This is how it works:

Loan (to purchase shares)	$100,000
Interest expense	($8,000)
Cash dividend	$4,000
Tax credits payable	$1,000
For a tax loss	($3,000)
Tax refund (at 34%)	$1,020
For a total cash flow loss	**($1,980)**

In this example, we're looking at a tax rate of 34%. But the tax refund rises to $1,395 for a tax payer in the top tax bracket (financial year 2013), to a cash flow loss of $1,605.

Assuming a long-term[3] average capital growth rate of 8%, the shares will grow to a value of $108,000 in a year (compounding), gaining $8,000 in value that will never be taxed until the shares are eventually sold (if ever). Even then they'll be taxed at a concessional rate (because outside of superannuation, when an asset is held for longer than 12 months, capital gains are only taxed at half the rate).

Not a bad scenario, is it?

A minor cash flow loss at worst (in this example, meaning it's only costing you $1,980 to borrow to buy the shares instead of $8,000), and when you consider the conservative annual capital growth rate of 8%, over time you're making significant gains. Added to this, your dividends are likely to increase, the debts will eventually be repaid, and before you know it you'll have sufficient equity and income to invest all over again.

---

3 This is the key with share investing! It must be for the long term, because short-term fluctuations will cause financial distraction like no other!

Diversity is the key

Companies can collapse. If you're an investor and your portfolio is spread equally over 25 *different* companies, then it's a hit you can take and still stay standing (and that really is almost a part of everyday share investing). If you're *not* diversified, though, and only hold shares in two companies, then if one fails you've just lost half your capital!

Index managed funds that track an index of a parcel of listed shares offer diversity in just one transaction at a low cost. And the most fantastic form of diversified, tax-efficient, dividend-paying, index-based share fund (and one ideally suited to negative gearing), is what's called an Exchange Traded Fund (ETF).

This is one of my favourite forms of 'easy' investment (which you can read more about in the Shares are Safer than Property chapter).

By buying shares in an ETF[4], you're diversifying within the one fund, which may (for example) be the entire ASX200.

This represents instant risk diversification without the time or costs involved in researching and monitoring a whole share portfolio! It really is brilliant!

You simply replace the word 'share' with the word 'ETF' (of your choice) and you too can be off and running as a negatively-geared investor.

The added bonus here is that you now have many other forms of tax savings open to you. For example, prepaying the interest on the loan in years when you're earning more, dividend imputation franking credits, claims for computer usage, light, power, internet usage, newspapers and finance magazines, travel, study, in fact anything at all that relates to your investments.

---

4 One major difference between index funds and ETF Index funds is that ETFs are bought and sold like any other share on the market.

It's entirely legitimate and totally legal.

Wow!

While we all need to pay tax to maintain our social standards and to provide a safety net for the very poor (which is why paying tax is not only a duty but actually a good thing for us all), minimising your taxes ethically and legally to assist funding longer-term capital growth is a 'norm' that is embraced by our taxation system.

So if you think you may be coming down with a bout of 'tax jealousy', call the tax doctor for a very palatable remedy.

Again, apologies for the literary licence, but I had to at least *try* to make a chapter about tax a little bit more interesting (and who said accountants aren't funny?).

CHAPTER SIX

BAD DEBT, GOOD DEBT

Debt is a massive financial distraction.

In fact, it's one of our biggest worries, and something we work the hardest to remove (pay off) and make the most sacrifices for.

The question to answer is, though, can bad debt be converted into good debt? Can we reduce our debt worries and pay off debt faster?

The answer is mostly 'yes', but let's get some background first.

We commonly hear the terms good debt and bad debt. Good debt is described as debt against investments, because we can offset (tax deduct) the interest expense against the income. Bad debt is debt against things we can't claim for (a tax deduction).

An example of good debt involves debt against a share portfolio, a rental property, or any other class of investment asset. An example of bad debt includes your home mortgage along with your car loan, credit card debts and personal loans.

But is any debt ever good?

The answer is 'yes' with investments, but (and I repeat *but*) only if the capital value growth or the income from the investment exceeds the costs.

Let's look at an example.

> *You have a rental property worth $400,000 and annually you pay $24,000 in interest on the loan, together with other costs totalling $3,000, while the rent you receive is $18,000, which means you're losing $9,000 in cash each and every year (excluding tax refunds and depreciation claims, which improve the outcome).*

In this simple, non-compounding example, if the property price doesn't rise by more than $90,000 over a 10-year period, is this debt a good debt? The answer is 'no'.

History shows us, however, that prices rise with inflation and population demand growth, and in all likelihood the property's value will grow by significantly more than $90,000, so the debt is classed as good debt. There is always a risk, of course, that history won't repeat itself and there are always unexpected variables that may crop up, so never do anything without thinking through all the possible outcomes, both good and bad.

Negative gearing, neutral gearing and positive gearing

Using the same example (again ignoring compounding and depreciation, because I cover this in quite a bit of detail later on), the $9,000 we're losing each year is called negative gearing, which can reduce the tax we have to pay.

Tax loss	($9,000)
Tax refund at 34%	$3,060
For a cash flow loss	**($5,940)**

In this example, we've used a tax rate of 34%. The tax saving rises to $4,185 for a tax payer in the top tax bracket for 2013.

Repeating the same example, let's assume the expenses are lower at $20,000 and the rent received is higher at $20,000. This is called neutral gearing.

Tax loss	$0
Tax refund at 34%	$0
Cash flow loss	**$0**

In this example, we're still using a tax rate of 34%, and the tax saving on zero is still zero for a tax payer in the top tax bracket for 2013.

Now let's assume the rent is $22,000 and the expenses are still $20,000. This is called positive gearing.

Tax profit	$2,000
Tax bill at 34%	($680)
Cash flow gain	**$1,320**

In this example, we're also using a tax rate of 34%, and the cash flow gain falls to $1,070 for a tax payer in the top tax bracket for 2013.

Interest only

You'll often hear people talk about good debt as being an interest only loan (especially while you've got bad debt or are saving for something that needs bad debt to fund it, like a holiday), but there's a bit more to it than that.

So what does 'good debt' actually mean?

Putting it simply, the interest on bad debts is paid for in *after* tax money.

In other words, let's say you earn $100 and pay $34 in tax (at the rate paid by your average tax payer). This leaves you with only $66 with which to repay your interest bill.

Interest on good debts is paid for in *before* tax money.

This is called good debt because the interest expense is tax deductible, which means you effectively have $100 with which to repay you interest bill or fund your debts.

The logic is simple enough.

Pay interest only on 'good debt' (investments), because you *can* claim the interest expense against your taxable income, and pay off 'bad debt' (home loans, personal loans, and credit cards), because that's not tax deductible and you *can't* claim the interest expense against your taxable income.

Knowing what you know now, why on earth would you pay off good debt before bad debt?

Debt recycling

Debt recycling involves converting bad debt into good debt. In other words, converting debt you *can't* claim a tax deduction for into debt you can.

Let's look at an example.

> *Over the years you've accumulated a share portfolio with a value of $100,000 with no debt attached to it. You also have a mortgage on a home totalling $400,000.*

An important point to consider is that you can't structure things purely to gain a tax benefit (and I'll talk more about this in a moment). There must always be some other benefit involved, no matter how minor. In this example, all the debt is tied up in the home.

One answer here is to re-structure the debt so as to re-weight the share portfolio and provide some simple asset protection by spreading the debt burden.

To achieve this, we'll sell the shares and reduce the mortgage, and then look at reborrowing to fund a new investment (to replace the share portfolio or to make some other investment, which is also often referred to as a separate line of credit, but remember, it must be interest only).

One major point of consideration when it comes to this example is tax. Selling the share portfolio may attract capital gains tax, so let's work through this as an example in action.

For the sake of the example, let's say we can take out a $100,000 loan at 6%, costing $6,000 per annum.

$100,000 share portfolio is sold and paid into the mortgage
$400,000 mortgage decreases to $300,000
$6,000 per annum, non-tax deductible interest expense is saved
$100,000 is now reborrowed (interest only) to buy a new share portfolio
$6,000 per annum, fully tax deductible interest expense is incurred
$2,040 annual tax saving

In this example, we're using a tax rate of 34%. The saving rises to $2,790 for a tax payer in the top tax bracket for 2013.

Consider another, not so happy example.

> *You own a home outright (no debt) worth $500,000. You're considering buying a new home to live in, while keeping and renting out your existing home. While you may be able to restructure the loan against the old property, the tax office won't*

allow you to claim the interest expense.

The previous $2,040 tax saving (on $100,000) becomes a $10,200 (on $500,000) annual loss.

In this example, we're using a tax rate of 34%. The loss rises to $13,950 for a tax payer in the top tax bracket for 2013.

Capital gains tax is the real consideration here. By selling the share portfolio, let's say you incur an initial capital gains tax bill of $5,000. The clawback period (the time it takes you to effectively get your money back), given you're saving $2,040 per year, is approximately two and half years. At the same time, you've also increased your cost base due to this initial amount of capital gains tax you've paid, meaning you'll be facing a smaller capital gains tax bill the next time you sell the shares for a (hopefully) higher capital gain.

The words 'no brainer' come to mind right at this point.

Remember my earlier word of warning, though. You can't enter into a scheme specifically for the purpose of obtaining a tax benefit.[5] Restructuring your affairs as part of normal practice, however, is perfectly acceptable, so see an advisor to ensure your reasoning is sound.

5 You can read Part IVA of the Income Tax Act, which is the general anti-avoidance rule when it comes to income tax, if you want to learn more about what this means.

CHAPTER SEVEN

SHARES ARE SAFER THAN PROPERTY

A major financial distraction for a lot of people derives from the seemingly endless debate over the investment value of shares verses property, especially when this is combined with the worry of holding shares during volatile periods on the share market.

While most of us prefer to simply hold property because we think it's less risky, others worry about being balanced investors and are distracted by their choices.

In this chapter, I'm going to try to overcome the reluctance when it comes to shares as an investment category, and bring a bit of balance back into the debate for those concerned about which path to go down. The reality is that we should invest in more than one category of asset, because having blind faith in only one category (even a category that's performed well in the past) is just plain madness.

The saying 'don't put all your eggs in one basket' represents sage advice indeed (and advice I've always taken seriously, given this author also holds residential, rural and commercial properties as well as shares).

Conflicts of interest

Right at the outset, I want to talk about an important consideration that involves the sources of possible bias involved with shares and associated margin lending (which simply involves the lending of money to invest in shares):

- Firstly, brokers have a vested interest in margin lending (the more shares or the more diversified a portfolio, the more they manage/earn).
- Bankers have a vested interest in margin lending, as they charge 2% to 3% more for this type of facility, and won't do it unless you offer personal guarantees (which includes all your other assets by default, and that includes your family home).
- Product providers (financial packagers) have fee-based vested interests.
- Financial planners are generally restricted to 'inside the square' products by their Dealer Group Licensee or can only advise on 'vanilla'-style margin lending with top Australian Stock Exchange (ASX) listed shares.[6]
- Options brokers are rare, and it's equally rare to find one that thinks outside the transactional square.

Before I alienate any of these well-meaning professionals, as most are highly professional advisors with your very best interests at heart, please remember that I'm speaking from a bean counter's perspective. And while accountants can't give formal financial advice specific to an individual's needs, they can certainly do the numbers on investments, and let you decide the risk/return equation for yourself.

---

6 Dealer groups hold Australian Financial Services Licences (AFSL) that financial planners belonging to the group are authorised to use.

So let's begin to question why we consider residential property 'safe'.

Current evidence suggesting residential property isn't the best investment is surprisingly strong. Any asset class carries risk, and while the last two decades (depending on what research you read) have seen at least two property booms, are we going to see the same thing over the next two decades?

The greatest risk with property is that its capital value stagnates or only slowly increases.

To illustrate, let's consider an example.

> *You have a rental property worth $400,000 and pay $24,000 in interest (6%) on the loan, and have other costs that total $3,000. The rent you receive each year is $18,000, so you're losing $9,000 in cash every year (excluding tax refunds and depreciation claims, which may or may not improve the outcomes).*

In this example, if the property price does not rise (or even falls) over a 10-year period, was this a safe investment? Now add combined transactional costs of another $50,000 to buy (stamp duty, etc) and sell (agent's fees, etc). Over the same 10-year period, it's fair to assume major repairs or just maintenance issues will occur at some point (let's say $10,000).

Was this property a safe investment?

Now, instead of losing the $9,000 in cash every year (not including the major repairs), let's assume this amount is invested elsewhere. Depending on how it's calculated, the compounded return (at the same 6%) accumulating over a 10-year period totals approximately $125,000, and by doing absolutely nothing at all.

Was this property still a safe investment?

Some logic?

The Master Builders Association (of Victoria) recently stated that historical housing affordability in Australia's capital cities has been at a ratio of 3:1. This means that the median house price was three times the median household income. Feel free to check the latest data when reading this book, but it's more likely to be double that figure at the time of writing, which is highly overpriced historically.

Now let's compare this to the share market.

The share market nudged 7,000 points in 2008 before the global financial crisis began and at the time of writing hovers at around 4,500 points.

Using simple logic (considering whether shares and property track at the same rate of capital return over time), the share market is currently well down historically when compared to property prices, which are historically high.

But which one has more room to move upwards in the future? Which one is safer?

Shane Oliver, head of investment strategy and chief economist at AMP Capital Investors, once made reference to the fact that the earliest he could get total return data for housing (capital growth plus rental yield) from the Real Estate Institute of Australia was from March 1983 (onwards). From this data, Oliver said that over the period March 1983 to December 2009, capital growth from residential property had been 8% per year, and after net rents the total return was 10.9% per year.[7]

Of course, this makes no allowance for property's high transactional costs. This lack of yield (rent income) in real estate, net 3% (usually found in capital cities), and the high costs to hold (for

7 Dunn, James. "Class Divide: Property vs Shares." The Australian 28 July. 2010.

example, land tax, periods of vacancy, re-letting fees, rates, repairs or just simply a bad tenant) is particularly highlighted when compared to share dividend yields of 4.5% that often also come with tax credits.

Shane Oliver also said that over the same period, Australian shares experienced a capital growth of 8.8% per year. Allowing for dividends, the total return was 13.3% per year (though this also excludes the very low 'shopped around' transactional costs).

So the results are certainly in when it comes to shares versus property over the period 1983 to 2009.

Shares win!

Transactional costs

The very high (ridiculously high, in fact) transactional costs involved with property (for example, stamp-duty, titles, conveyancing, agent selling fees on disposal, marketing, etc), escalate the costs of buying and selling real estate to around 10% or more.

As a result, buying, selling and holding property costs plenty when compared with buying and selling shares, so you have to also consider what the real net returns are after including these transactional costs.

Let's pause for some balance

Investment is all about diversification. Property is a very good investment, especially if it's the family home, commercial premises for your own business, rural interests, or a well researched residential investment. The whole point of this chapter is not to knock property as a good potential investment, but to debunk the perception that property is safer and enjoys better returns than shares.

When comparing property and share investing, the big difference in terms of safety is that you **can** *protect the value of shares by hedging (also called capital protection), but you can't easily protect the value of property.*

There are two ways of hedging shares, either via a packaged product or directly through the market. Hedging isn't often considered, though, and a 2011 survey by Wealth Insights into the reasons advisers don't use hedging products found that 46% of them thought they are too expensive and 27% thought they were too complicated.[8] Capital protection, however, is an important part of prudent investing and should form a part of every investment share portfolio.

It is often said that time is the best capital protection there is. The problem is that recovering value lost in a downturn can take a very long time, not to mention the fact that market crashes can also come at precisely the *wrong* time (on retirement, for example), especially with highly leveraged investments, where you simply may not have the time to spare. And what happens if the world heads into a long period of recession or a depression?

The protection afforded by just waiting things out may not be realistic.

Capital protection does come at a price, though (but so does not being protected if and when things don't go as expected). At a cost of around 6% to 8% per year to fully protect a portfolio, these costs decrease to around 3% to protect a market fall of 8% to 10% and 1.5% to protect a fall of 10% to 15%. By using other strategies that I'll talk about later in the chapter (relating to call options and covered call options), these costs can be reduced even further or even eliminated altogether (free insurance!).

8 Taylor, Mike. "Advisors Shun Capital Protection." Money Management 10 June. 2011.

Exchange Traded Funds

Exchange Traded Funds (or ETFs) are simply investment funds that are traded on the stock exchange. An ETF invests in a basket of securities (or other assets) that generally seeks to track the performance of a specified index or benchmark (like the S&P/ASX 200 index).

As accountants, we just love ETFs! It's share market investing for busy people, or people with no interest in watching or learning about individual shares on the market, and all at a very low cost.

By buying one share in an ETF (for example, the SPDR S&P/ ASX 200 FUND, with the stock code: STW) you're actually buying all of the top 200 shares listed on the ASX. The company collects the dividends for you and passes them out twice a year.

It's that simple (and cheap).

There is some argument about which approach offers the better returns: simply buying a balanced share portfolio like an ETF and sitting on it (passive investment), or trying to pick the market highs and lows and trading around these (active investment).

For most of us, unless you're a share tragic, passive investment will likely win out every time.

Margin lending

I'm really only covering margin lending here for the sake of being thorough. The reality is that margin lending products are frankly a bit of a joke, and that's because of the cost of capital.

Where the market may pay you a 6% dividend return (including tax credits), the cost to do this through margin lending is currently around 9%. The result is that you're losing 3% each and every year unless you have capital growth, and a great deal more if the market crashes.

Call options

There are other alternatives to margin lending, of course, one of which is the humble 'call' option.

Putting it simply, an option is a contract between two parties that gives the option buyer (called the 'taker') the right, but not the obligation, to buy (called a 'call') or sell (called a 'put') a security for a particular price on or before a particular date. The buyer pays a premium to the option seller (called the 'writer') of the contract.

Interestingly, call options are often considered too complex to easily use (and margin lending isn't complex?). The reason why, though, is largely due to education (or lack thereof) and licensing issues.

The reality, however, is actually quite the opposite.

There is nothing simpler to transact than a call option, and give me a minute or two with even the direst of know-nothings when it comes to matters of finance, and they'll know all there is to know about them.

A call option (which you'll pay a premium for) basically gives you the right to buy a security at a given price within a given period of time.

Two of the option contract classes traded on the Australian Stock Exchange are share option contracts and index option contracts.

Share option contracts involve individual company shares, and the standard number of shares covered is 100 (although this can change for a number of different reasons). This basically means one option contract will represent 100 underlying shares.

Index option contracts involve a particular market index and offer exposure to a range of shares (rather than being limited to a particular company). The contract value in this case is based on a dollar value per index point.

There are other important differences between these two option classes, and I always recommend my clients visit the Australian Stock Exchange website for more detailed information (and certainly more detail than I'll be going into here).[9]

Now let's look at an example.

> *Let's say you buy a 4,500 index call option for a premium of say \$360*[10] *(plus brokerage and exchange fees) for the year. This gives you the right to 'own' the market (to make money, basically) when the index reaches 4,500 points.*
>
> *If the market finishes above 4,860 points by the end of the year, you make a profit.*
>
> *If the market finishes at 4,700 points by the end of the year, then you at least get back \$200 of your \$360 dollars.*
>
> *And if the market crashes, then the most you can lose is \$360.*

Option prices are based on current volatility, and at the time of writing, the market was a lot less volatile than the example here implies.

The whole point is that for a cost of 8% (of your investment's value) per year, you can fully protect your investment with no financing costs (but also no dividends). And these costs decrease to around 3% per year to protect against a market fall of 10%, which is the equivalent of margin lending with no margin calls (and just ask anyone whether they think margin calls hurt).

If the market crashes 20%, then you can re-buy the call option at the new low point and recover faster from that position than you can

---

9 www.asx.com.au.

10 This hypothetical index option has a premium of 36 points at \$10 per point.

using the margin lending alternative, which has to claw its way back 20% to its cost base before you're back to actual capital growth again.

Covered call options

This strategy is talked about a lot, and when used wisely is also very good.

In the traditional sense, a covered call option involves a situation where you already own shares and sell the right to someone else to buy those shares at a certain price (called the 'strike' price, which will be higher than your shares' current price).

A wise strategy when it comes to covered call options involves not doing anything at all whenever the market is down, and just be patient. Wait for market highs and *then* sell your covered calls.

If you simply pursue a strategy of doing it every month regardless, though, in all likelihood you'll eventually be burnt.

Call options and covered call options are something you need to understand and come to grips with, and sitting down with an advisor is often the best way. Once again, make your starting point a visit to the Australian Stock Exchange's website.

Borrowing costs

In the good old days, capital protection costs were tax deductible. Today this has mostly gone, and protection costs are capitalised. Similarly, when you're borrowing to buy a call option (for example), the premium is non-deductible if it's just a buy and hold strategy (capitalised).

Protection costs do become deductible, however, if there's an expectation of income. For example, if you're planning to regularly sell covered call options against your own call options then this certainly represents an expectation of income and with a ruling from the ATO (which is simple for your accountant to prepare), the interest is once again tax deductible.

Capital growth

Whether it's property or shares, investments lose money in the holding stage, and if there's no capital growth then there's no point owning the investment, even if it's saving you from having to pay some tax.

As an accountant, it never ceases to amaze me how much money people will throw away just to save a few dollars in tax. The highest possible tax rate is around 46%, which means if you want to save $46 dollars in tax, you first need to spend $100! And this is pointless unless you have at least a potential for capital growth exceeding the $54 difference between the tax and the expense.

Sometimes it's simply best to stay cashed up, be ready, and just wait for the right moment.

Recognising the right moment is the tricky bit, of course, so talk to an expert and put your strategy in place.

SUMMING IT ALL UP

When I first started in the accounting business, my mentor was a seasoned and successful share ambassador (he also held properties; balance, remember!) and we had a share market dip to deal with.

All the clients were ringing us, asking for our advice in the face of a 20% loss in value.

In each case he simply replied, "Have you sold them?"

When they inevitably replied in the negative, he said, "Well then, you haven't lost anything, have you?"

Time and time again he's been proven right, as diversified shares bounce back and values return. Shares will always be more volatile, because we see the data reacting every second to market sentiment, but if we take a longer-term view (as we do in property) then traditionally the volatility evens out.

This chapter is aimed at easing the worry and the financial distraction when it comes to share investing. But remember, this writer also owns residential, commercial and rural property, so the key point is also all about keeping your finances and investments balanced.

CHAPTER EIGHT

FARMING WITH SUPERANNUATION

Long-term rural investment is one great way to reduce your immediate financial distractions, with proven long-term rates of return on established practices, coupled with the capital growth of rural property, especially in productive areas with good rain and soil.

Farming with your self-managed superannuation fund (SMSF), especially if you have a general interest in all things rural, can be one of the most powerful ways to invest.

Additionally, and often by its very nature, the investment can work well as a double-edged taxation strategy. By double-edged, I mean that it maximises the tax concessions in terms of both superannuation and in a lot of different types of farming, especially when we're considering long lead times before seeing a profit (and forestry falls into this category in particular). This means you can receive significant up-front tax deductions coupled with a delayed income, which will often be taxed at a lower rate when it does commence, ultimately meaning less tax overall.

By using your superannuation rather than personal, non-superannuation equity to buy land you intend to commercially farm, you can free up that equity for other investments or even to fund the farming business itself. Even better, by using instalment warrants, your SMSF can even borrow to buy the land, again freeing up your equity.

You have a lot of options.

Let's begin this chapter by looking at how the Australian Tax Office (ATO), which regulates the administration of SMSFs as well as their taxation, defines a primary producer:

"You are a primary producer if you carry on a business of:

PLANT AND ANIMAL CULTIVATION

- cultivating or propagating plants, fungi or their products or parts (including seeds, spores, bulbs and similar things) in any physical environment
- maintaining animals for the purpose of selling them or their bodily produce, including natural increase
- manufacturing dairy produce from raw material that you produced.

FISHING AND PEARLING

- conducting operations relating directly to taking or catching fish, turtles, dugong, beche-de-mer, crustaceans or aquatic molluscs
- conducting operations relating directly to taking or culturing pearls or pearl shell.

TREE FARMING AND FELLING

- planting or tending trees in a plantation or forest that are intended to be felled
- felling trees in a plantation or forest
- transporting trees or parts of trees that you felled in a plantation or forest to the place
  - where they are first to be milled or processed

- from which they are to be transported to the place where they are first to be milled or processed."[11]

As they say, the very best way to show how a thing works is by example. So the example I'll be using is from an actual case involving tree farming.

Don't let yourself be put off by tree farming (I do it myself). It's a well-established and profitable enterprise whose reputation has only suffered as a result of a few big companies that sold ultimately doomed prospectus-based products.

In reality, the timber industry is both mature and well-proven.

Let's look at another example.

Your SMSF buys farm land for $400,000 and rents it back to you at an independently assessed commercial rate of $30,000 per annum (plus outgoings). Let's also assume you're on the average marginal tax rate of 34%.

Immediately, we have a tax arbitrage (which is the ability to take advantage of a difference in tax rates as the basis for profit) represented by a 34% deduction in your name (as the farmer) for the rent, and a tax rate of 15% on the income for the superannuation fund. This represents either a 19% tax saving or a real positive return of 19%, but no matter how you want to look at it, it's the same dollar outcome.

You now plant a tree plantation in your own name on your SMSF's land, with the planting spread over three financial years at a total cost of $200,000, using your own subcontracted forester to do the work. At a taxation rate of 34%, this enables

11 Australian Tax Office. Available http://www.ato.gov.au/businesses/PrintFriendly.aspx?ms=businesses&doc=/content/33519.htm. Viewed 10 August 2012.

you to claim personal tax refunds/deductions of $68,000 but (there are a series of commercial business tests you'll need to pass to be able to do so, which I'll talk about later in this chapter).

From our example, some other tax deductions that are possible over time involve ongoing annual expenses, including the rent you're now paying to your SMSF (which is also a great way to get more funds into your superannuation fund), insurance, interest on loans (if borrowed) and the ongoing costs from planting and maintaining the trees.

And this is a terrific point to share a tax tip when it comes to income and deductions. If you're facing a year where you're anticipating a significant burst of income (from a large capital gain, for example) that will push you into the top tax bracket (46.5%), the total tax refund/deduction from our example rises to $93,000, so it's very important to get the timing of your investments just right.

Importantly, with this timing we're claiming tax deductions while the plantation grows, in financial years well before when we'll be expecting to receive income from the harvest.

When we do harvest, ideally it will be later, during the usually more relaxed working years just prior to retirement, when we're still able to maximise superannuation contributions and minimise the plantation income.

Ideally, you don't harvest the whole plantation in one year, but spread it out (or at least the income from it) over two or more years while other income (and therefore your tax rate) is lower, again picking up once more on tax arbitrage.

As we discuss in more detail later on, your own superannuation fund can also borrow if necessary (through a simple instalment warrant) to buy into the farming land.

Here are a couple of examples of how farming works.

> *Your SMSF buys farm land and rents it back to you to farm beef cattle. There's no difference here from the previous examples, except the income commences a lot sooner from the sale of the cattle.*
>
> *Your SMSF buys farm land and rents it back to you for broadacre crop farming. You can even live on part of the farm while tending to your fields. Once again, there's no real difference with this example, other than the relative speed of the income from the crop.*

Just don't forget that we have two very different entities here—you and your SMSF—with two totally different income streams—the SMSF's rental income and your income from the crop yield (for example)—and altogether different tax treatments—your SMSF attracts only 0% to 15%, while you attract the normal rate on income that all taxpayers face, which requires traditional tax planning to maximise your returns (such as contributions to super, wages to family members when working in the business, and normal capital asset depreciation and write-offs).

By now I hope you're getting a feel for how this works. As with all genuine, ATO-approved primary production businesses where there is a need or it is normal practice to do so, you can also live on small parts of your SMSF's farmland while tending its operation, and I'll talk about this in detail a little later in this chapter.

So why farmland?

It's my belief (backed by plenty of experience) that farm land is generally too cheap, and for the simple reason that it will be in significant demand in the future. Think about supply and demand and the effects of a growing population in Australia.

In my opinion, sooner or later, our various carbon emission reduction schemes will start to drive demand for land, by forcing major corporations into buying up farmland for carbon offsets. The day is coming and it'll bring the established international carbon market along with it.

Food production will be an ongoing issue as the world's population grows and farm usage faces increasing competition from lifestyle demands as cities become more crowded and seek to expand. Additionally, banks are currently lending less on rural land after the global financial crisis. Like all boom/bust cycles, however, this will eventually end, allowing people to be able to borrow more freely once again.

All of this will contribute to higher rural land prices in the future.

Why superannuation?

Rural land is almost a perfect match for superannuation investment, simply because it is a long-term investment. With the recent poor performance from managed superannuation, there is a lot of general reluctance about putting funds into superannuation. The do-it-yourself superannuation options, however, have been booming, as the available superannuation tax concessions simply can't be ignored, and for many of us, SMSFs provide a more acceptable way to access them.

Under our current laws, pre-tax contributions to superannuation provide the most tax-effective strategy we have. By simply investing in superannuation, you can make a 19% return on pre-tax money if you're in the 34% tax bracket (the equivalent at the time of writing of around four years term deposit interest), or a 31.5% return if you're in the top tax bracket.

Let's look at another example of how this difference works.

Assume you pay tax at the 34% tax rate and have surplus savings of around $200 per week after tax ($303 before tax). Ordinarily you'd lose $103 in tax each week. Alternatively, if you salary sacrifice directly into superannuation, you lose only $45 per week in tax. That's a savings difference of $58 each and every week, week after week.[12]

Don't forget, with superannuation the tax-effective savings don't stop at the contributions level, as superannuation earnings are only taxed at 10% to 15%, and after retiring it gets even better, as the earnings attract an unbelievable tax rate of zero percent! Further, the tax paid on superannuation payouts after the age of sixty (and retired or semi-retired) is again zero (in most cases, but remember, individual circumstances vary, so always get independent advice)!

Borrowing with your super

Since the ATO's clarification in September 2007, SMSFs have really been borrowing to buy property on their own behalf, through the prudent use of easily constructed instalment warrants.

An instalment warrant is a form of derivative and I'm very well placed to provide advice about the benefits of their use, having done a doctorate on them.

Let's look at another example, this time considering a simple strategy using instalment warrants.

> *Let's say you put $200,000 into your own SMSF, which then borrows a further $200,000 through an instalment trust structure and buys a farm for forestry. You can rent the land back to either yourself or an investor, making the investment*

12 The catch is you can't get to this money until you retire at fifty-five or sixty (depending on your age now).

cash-flow positive, which with your 9% superannuation payroll contributions and any additional salary sacrifices will help pay down the loan even faster.

There are numerous strategies you can pursue (well beyond the simple examples we're briefly covering here) that can substantially enhance your returns. For example, you can consider getting together with friends in a geared unit trust to buy a larger block, providing significantly enhanced economies of scale. Alternatively, you can finance the purchase of units in a unit trust yourself, to avoid gearing inside the trust.

Whatever you decide to do, you must always talk to your financial advisor, who will have plenty of other tax-effective ideas.

Tax laws and deductions

An ATO concern when it comes to primary production involves satisfying a series of non-commercial loss-deductibility tests, which is something you'll need to discuss with an accountant prior to embarking on any agri-investment.

While this may all appear quite daunting, relax. Accountants deal with them regularly, and as long as the primary production activity is an independently verifiable venture, then there are usually no issues whatsoever.

The income requirement and business tests

The first non-commercial loss-deductibility test involves being able to offset a business loss (this chapter focuses on primary production, but the tests are the same for any other business loss) against other income, which means you need to satisfy the following tests.

The income requirement test

Your income must be less than $250,000. This $250,000 is not just your taxable income (per your tax assessment) but also includes:

- business losses
- total reportable fringe benefits amounts
- additional reportable superannuation contributions
- total net investment losses.

Even if you're 'lucky' enough to fail the $250,000 test (meaning you have income above $250,000), you can apply for a private ruling on the exercise of the Commissioner of Taxation's discretion to allow the loss offsets. The basis for the Commissioner's discretion includes:

- special circumstances outside your control (high income from an unusual event, like receipt of a large insurance payout from fire, flood, and even drought)
- the nature of the activity, for example when there are long lead times before a tax profit (tree farming for instance)
- an objective expectation based on independent evidence (via an independent report) that a profit will be made in a time that is normal for the industry.

Once the Commissioner's discretion has been granted, then the losses are fully claimable against your ordinary income.

The business tests

If you have an adjusted income below $250,000, then passing one of these next four business tests is essential to be able to offset the losses:

- **The assessable income test**, where the business activity has assessable income of at least $20,000.
- **The profits test**, where the business had a profit for tax

purposes in three out of the past five years (including the current year).

- **The real property test**, where the value of real property (or of an interest in real property) that you used in the business on a continuing basis was at least $500,000.
- **The other assets test**, where the value of assets (excluding real property, cars, motor cycles and similar vehicles) you used on a continuing basis in carrying on the business was at least $100,000.

If our primary production activity doesn't pass one of these four tests, then an application can be made for the Commissioner's discretion in the exact same way as for the income requirement test.

Remember, a viable venture only needs to qualify for the Commissioner's discretion once, and for the life of the project the discretion will usually apply.

Finally, there is one other exemption to note for primary production losses. Where other non-primary production adjusted income is less than $40,000 and excludes capital gains from the calculation, you're able to offset the losses without question.

In-house assets restrictions

The final issue to address involves in-house assets restrictions, which generally prevent an SMSF's members from effectively investing in themselves (or associated entities).

This doesn't, however, apply to farms or business property.

For example, our SMSF can own a farm that may also have a farm house on it that you're allowed to use, as long as it's for the daily management/maintenance of the farm or tending the crops while you're leasing the farmland back to the SMSF member.

As long as that part of the farmland is no larger than two hectares, then there are no regulatory issues. The catch is, though, that the property's purpose **must** be for farming, which means no part of it may be used by you for private or domestic purposes (for example by also taking the family there for holidays or other recreation).

When your super is involved, it's all work and no play.

SUMMING IT ALL UP

The results from combining superannuation, agri-business and farming land are well worth the effort, and simply too good to be ignored.

1. Get advice in the first instance and get it quickly. Speak to a farmer or forester and an SMSF expert.
2. Maximise the super power of superannuation. Why? Because it's yours, it's protected, it has so many tax advantages, and it will be instrumental in accelerating your wealth through farming opportunities. Why accelerate wealth? Because wealth gives you choices, which is always a good thing.
3. Superannuation offers fantastic opportunities:
   - Immediate tax-effective returns on your contributions.
   - Concessional (low) tax rates on the earnings.
   - Tax-free status at age sixty for most (and semi-retired/retired).
   - The ability to borrow.

The primary production rules are full of traps and superannuation rules often change from year-to-year, but this is nothing to be intimidated by, just understood and complied with.

You do need to speak with your accountant (and I cannot emphasise this enough), or do your own research prior to undertaking any tax-effective investment opportunities based on the primary production activities described in this chapter.

CHAPTER NINE

ILLNESS AND DEATH

I'm going to open this chapter with a bit of a warning. I'll be addressing issues that many people prefer to avoid (and I tend to count myself in this group). The fact remains, however, that we all need to face up to the reality of both illness and death, even if reluctantly.

We all know people who have been touched by serious illnesses, death and even both, and yet at heart we're all a strange kind of optimist (well most of us), preferring to push events like that aside on the basis that they won't happen to us.

Although the likelihood of injury at home or work is thankfully reasonably low, what if it happens and we're unprepared? The reality is that even while most of us think it won't happen, there's often a niggling doubt, an almost unconscious concern that something will.

The good news is that this form of financial distraction is extremely easy to address before it happens. The bad news is that it's a nightmare with consequences to address once it has and you've done nothing beforehand.

If we have a road-based accident, the compulsory insurance we all pay as part of our registration premiums will cover medical and income to some extent. This is the same with workplace accidents, which are usually covered by an employer (however, non-employees or the self-employed are not necessarily covered under the same policies), but the death or trauma payouts of both are likely to be insufficient to protect the family in most cases and still need to be reviewed.

The risk really arises from accidents that are not car or work-related and of course illnesses. We all need to at least look at how and where we're covered and address it as needed.

While some people may already have insurance to cover death, loss of income, and trauma-related events via their employer, and others may elect to take out private insurance either personally or through their own business, the majority of us have either very limited insurance or none at all.

So let's begin by first looking at some of the major insurance protections.

Insurance protection

Most of us wouldn't drive a car without insurance (even if it's just third party) and most of us wouldn't own a home without insuring that, just as most of us will insure jewellery as part of the household contents.

Yet, when it comes to our most important asset, ourselves and our loved ones, we barely give the issue a second thought.

But there really are four main types of events we need to seriously consider insuring against.

Income protection protects your income if you're unable to work, providing you with a percentage of the income you were earning prior to the event.

Death insurance pays in case of death and is one of the cheapest forms of insurance available (especially if you're a non-smoker), and provides security for your dependents.

Trauma insurance pays if you are diagnosed with a major health problem, even if you fully recover from it. Consider you've just been diagnosed with cancer, and your trauma policy pays a $200,000 lump sum. Your recovery is going to be a whole lot less stressful if you know you can take the time off work to focus on healing and still be able to pay for the increased health bills.

Total permanent disability (TPD) insurance pays if you're permanently disabled and unable to return to work (for example, if a major stroke prevents you from ever working again).

Tax-effectiveness is something we always consider with the cost of insurance protection and how the premiums are paid. For example, with income protection it's relatively simple, as premiums are tax deductible against income, but the other three forms of insurance can be a little more complicated.

When paid other than by your superannuation fund, death and TPD insurance are not tax deductible (with some exceptions), and trauma insurance policies are rarely if ever deductible. However, death and TPD insurance can be made deductible in a roundabout way, by having your superannuation fund own the policies (and so becoming the insured party).

In effect, your superannuation fund pays the premiums and these payments can be made by either a self-managed superannuation fund, an industry-based fund, or a commercial fund (as nearly all these funds offer insurance of this type). So if cash flow is tight, this is often a good approach to explore, especially if you'll otherwise be without insurance at all.

If you have sufficient cash flow, you can consider making extra contributions to your superannuation fund (over and above your normal compulsory work place contributions) to pay for the premiums. When done correctly, these additional payments are tax deductible, and importantly, your superannuation funds will not be depleted by the cost of the insurance premiums.

Trauma insurance is rarely deductible. If you ever have to claim, however, the payout is usually tax free, and the significant likelihood of a trauma event occurring prior to age sixty-five makes holding this type of protection a very serious consideration.

The next key point to make is that while a household's breadwinner is usually the one insured, the lower income spouse is generally not.

Personally, I think this is madness.

In this situation, think about what happens if the lower income spouse is traumatised, chronically disabled, or prematurely dies. Generally, the breadwinner is going to have to move to shorter hours or even stop work altogether. Clearly, it's just as important to have both spouses covered.

The next consideration here involves family breakdowns (which unfortunately are all too common). After a breakdown, one spouse may be at home looking after the children and relying on income from child support to raise them. Now imagine the outcome if the child-support paying spouse is traumatised, chronically disabled, or dies?

The value of these insurance types is all too obvious when you really start to think about it.

One other insurance type to address is health insurance. Most people don't value it, but will want it rather than having to wait (or pay) for non-essential health intervention in the public system if the event arose.

There are two issues with health insurance.

Firstly, if you're over age thirty and don't have it, the premium surcharge increases each year that you don't. As a result, later on in life when you're most likely to need it, you may not be able to afford it.

Secondly, if you're a higher income earner without health insurance, you may be paying an additional tax penalty, so review your position on health insurance with your tax accountant.

Testamentary trusts

A testamentary trust (or a will trust) is a type of trust (normally discretionary and controlled by a trustee) created by your will that comes into effect when you die. Intended to 'control the estate from the grave', your estate is paid into the testamentary trust, instead of being distributed directly to your will's beneficiaries.

When I use the term 'control', I don't necessarily mean it in a negative way. Sometimes a will of this type can be essential when, for example, there are handicapped children involved, or children from a previous marriage, or maybe a drug-addicted sibling who's at risk of frittering a lump sum, or a spouse that will receive a large life insurance pay out and face income tax problems as a result.

There are a myriad of reasons, both good and bad, why a testamentary trust is sometimes better than leaving inheritances directly to beneficiaries.

Let's look at an example.

> *Let's say a wife is left $1,000,000 on a death-based policy to help raise the children, and she invests that money wisely. She'll be taxed on the earnings from that investment and can't put the money into the children's name to spread the tax load, even though it's essentially being used for their benefit. This is because of the penalty tax rates for minors when it comes to unearned income, which is an otherwise noble tax rule, but an extremely unfair one under these circumstances.*

If a testamentary trust is in place, the assets from the will pass through to the trust controlled by the surviving spouse (often as the trustee), and the income can then be spread among the children at normal adult tax rates (which are much lower).

For example, let's say there are two child beneficiaries. Each child can receive around $20,000 in income, tax free, which represents a much better tax outcome.

Death and divorce raises some interesting issues. As mentioned, what happens if a child-support paying spouse dies? Does the estate go to the ex-spouse? What happens if there's a new marriage involved or additional children? Who ends up receiving the benefit?

What if a previous spouse has been removed from the will and everything has been left to the child-support paying spouse's siblings who have been tasked to look after the children? Despite the trust (and burden) this arrangement relies on, what happens if the circumstances of those siblings change?

There are numerous risks involved with leaving an estate directly to the beneficiaries, and yet a simple testamentary trust can solve most of them.

If you're considering a testamentary trust, though, then you must have it in place *before* you die. It cannot be added once you're dead. It's a simple addition/mechanism attached to your will that can provide some phenomenal peace of mind.

Death taxes

Although they're not called death taxes here, we still have a form of death tax in Australia. For example, let's say we have a retired couple with two tax-free thresholds, joint pension thresholds, and joint tax rebates. When one partner dies, the remaining partner will usually have the same income, but now with only one set of thresholds, and so up go the tax liabilities. In some cases, a loss of pension soon follows.

There are so many cases where the loss of one partner is accompanied by a loss of benefits, and you need to plan for it. This is simply called estate planning, and you should have an estate plan even if it's just an outline of a strategy (rather than a full blown document addressing all matters in detail).

Estate planning is best considered before you die, but unlike a testamentary trust, some issues can still be addressed after death. The problem is that generally this is not the ideal time, especially when a death is recent and the remaining partner is still grieving. Given a testamentary trust can often form a part of the estate planning, it's essential that things are put in place before you die.

Another trap to be aware of is that if you've elected your spouse to be the recipient, when you die your superannuation passes to them and no tax penalties will usually apply. After the remaining spouse dies, however, and if that superannuation then passes to the children, then it *is* mostly taxed. The trick in this case is to pull all money out of superannuation completely tax free just before the remaining spouse dies, and gift it to the beneficiaries (or hold it in a bank account).

No-one knows their hour of death (so to speak), which makes it essential that if it hasn't been done beforehand, during estate planning, when one spouse dies, you must review the superannuation situation.

If we're considering the case of two elderly parents, then when one of them passes away, the estate normally goes to the surviving spouse. As mentioned, however, this may mean a loss of benefits. So in a case where the remaining spouse has little need for the money, then consider only paying out a portion of the estate (or more or less than half), instead of leaving it all to the surviving spouse.

Capital gains tax on property and shares can also be avoided on death by transferring assets to beneficiaries in probate rather than selling the assets, providing an ideal time (though what's ever ideal about death) to consider a tax-effective restructure.

SUMMING IT ALL UP

There is rarely a good time to consider these events. Being an accountant, however, means I witness these events and the lack of planning and the obvious financial disasters that result on an all-too-regular basis.

The reality is that these things happen. Addressing them prior to the event and having a plan in place makes the outcome for both you and your loved ones so much easier.

In fact, it's a matter of such a high priority that you should do it today.

CHAPTER TEN

DIVORCE

This is by far the biggest chapter in this book and for obvious reasons. With around forty percent of marriages ending up in divorce, and very few of them ending up in an amicable settlement, the financial distractions that come with divorce are simply enormous.

Having been through divorce myself, and through several hundred of them vicariously through my clients, I've come to realise that in nearly every case, the main stumbling block to achieving a timely and mutually agreeable settlement is a looming uncertainty about the financial future. Believe it or not, addressing this uncertainty at the outset can go an enormous way to making the whole process a lot smoother (if the word 'smooth' can ever be associated with divorce).

The three scenarios we run through–Divorced dads, mums and soloists–confront different financial distractions that are fundamentally not dissimilar, because they all face major changes and often need to address the same financial issues but on different time scales.

Divorced dads

Most dads make mistake after mistake with financial settlements and they need help. This part of the chapter is written specifically for divorced dads and the many challenges they face in their post-divorce recovery. I'll get to divorced mums and divorcees without dependents (the soloists) a little later on.

Regrettably, I can't patch up the differences that contributed to the end of a marriage, but what I can do is make sure that both parents and non-parents are afforded every opportunity to recover and achieve the best possible financial outcome.

There are a significant number of strategies dads can apply, which will marginalise the downside, make their recovery as fast as possible and ensure they can continue to provide for their children in the best possible way.

First, let's look at a common scenario for the typical divorced dad.

Sadly, a marriage ends. Let's say our mum, who we'll call Sue, receives 65% of the asset base, which normally includes the tax-free family home. Our dad, who we'll call Tim, typically receives a cash settlement or other assets, like a rental property, shares, or his superannuation, which once formed part of the marriage pool.

Tim's settlement earns interest, dividends, or rent that he has to pay tax on, which also increases his income for (after-tax) child maintenance payments, which will make those payments higher.

In an attempt to start again, a dad will usually buy a house to live in and so does Tim. Typically, house prices may have increased during the protracted separation process, and the deposit saved for the purchase comes from after-tax income. Tim's also up for stamp duty and all the associated costs of buying a new home.

Now Tim is being seriously stretched financially. He's facing new mortgage payments, which he has to work harder to meet, and the minute he starts doing that, he'll find himself paying more tax on the extra income, as well as having to make larger payments for child and quite possibly spousal maintenance (which just increases the more he earns). And that's on top of the whole new suite of costs he has to meet now he's living on his own.

Tim's trapped in a vicious circle, and he's going to struggle to escape it.

Divorce lawyers really aren't acting in the very best interests of their clients if they aren't across the intricacies of the tax/financial system, which comes as no surprise, considering it generally isn't their area of expertise. For example, try explaining to a divorced dad that while he got the rental property tax free at settlement, when he sells it, the tax liability doesn't go away. It's simply deferred and some day he's going to have to pay it.

Any divorce lawyer who doesn't instruct his or her client to seek separate tax and financial advice and to develop a plan for their post-settlement recovery *before accepting a settlement*, really needs to take a long hard look at whether they're looking after their client as well as they should be.

Most importantly, though, divorcing dads cope a whole lot better with what is often perceived to be a 'lousy' settlement if they have a financial plan for the future, and this can only make a divorce lawyer's job that little bit easier.

How to move on

The best way to move on financially is to latch on to a strategy that you believe in and can commit to. The simple fact is that you're not alone. There are many avenues for support and guidance. Make an appointment to see an adviser, get some direction and get going. There are always ways forward.

I nearly always recommend one of two basic roads to recovery:

1. If you're under fifty, look at buying a home and rebuilding your equity.
2. If you're over fifty, look at *safe* forms of superannuation while renting, or restructure your home loan (if you have one) to make interest-only repayments to free up cash flow to contribute to superannuation.

In either case, we can still consider a raft of other tax-effective investing strategies regardless of age or circumstances.

Get a roof over your head

When marriages break down and there are children involved, Dad is usually the one who moves out. On top of significant costs to establish a new home, he also begins to pay child maintenance and in some cases spousal maintenance, and it's only after these costs have been met that he can start funding a whole new round of costs on his own, including rent, electricity, water, gas, and the list goes on.

But here's my point: *all these outgoings are in after-tax dollars.*

In this respect, the tax system is working against you.

The inevitable asset split usually favours the child-rearing parent (and rightfully so) and the asset growth that the child-rearing parent enjoys is usually tax-free, given the asset is most likely going to be the family home.

Often, Dad is left without the family home and with a smaller capital base (which appreciates at a proportionally lower amount), and even then, any increase on that smaller capital base is often taxed.

The good news is that there are creative ways you can address this asset and taxation imbalance.

Superannuation is one very powerful method, given it's taxed on a concessional basis (15% at the time this book was written) with the implication being that when you reach the age of sixty and retire, the proceeds are totally tax-free in most cases.

Building equity is so important for the under fifties (and is still important for the over fifties with property). Banks love equity and will readily lend against it, affording you wealth-building opportunities along the way. Buying a home is important, but paying for a home in after-tax dollars after the age of fifty is often not the best approach. As compelling as it may seem to you, you'd have a hard time convincing me of the merits of a strategy like this when there are much better options available.

Let's look at some examples to illustrate the point.

You buy a home and rent it out rather than living in it, while keeping your own rent costs low, or even consider sharing a place with family, friends or a colleague.

By doing this you expose yourself to capital growth, which gets you back in the game. Any capital gain here will, unfortunately, be taxed upon sale. So if at all possible, don't sell, because you can leverage (borrow against) the unrealised capital gain (increase in value) to finance your next investment opportunity.

One other way to avoid the capital gain trap is to live in the house first and then for a period of six years after you've moved out, the property retains the capital gains tax exemption. The key is to make sure you move in first.

Alternatively, consider this approach using a superannuation investment strategy (described next) and avoid all tax on the sale in retirement!

Here's roughly how it works:

Loan for a house/unit	$400,000
Interest payable at 6%	($24,000)
Rates, repairs, body corporate, etc	($2,500)
Rent received	$19,500
For a cash flow loss	**($7,000)**

Now take into account the taxation considerations:

Non-cash chattel depreciation	$1,500
Non-cash building depreciation (2.5%)	$7,500
For a tax loss	**($16,000)**
Tax refund on the tax loss (at 34%)	**$5,440**
Total cash flow loss	**($1,560)**

In this example we're looking at a tax rate of 34%. But the tax saving rises to $7,440 for a tax payer in the top tax bracket (financial year 2013), to a $440 cash flow gain!

Not a bad scenario, is it?

A minor cash flow loss at worst and if you consider even a conservative capital growth rate of 5%, this equates to $20,000 per annum compounding on your $400,000 property. Over time, rents will increase, debts will slowly be repaid, and the gap between $20,000 in annual growth and your net expenses continues to grow, as does your ability to invest all over again.

So, where to from here?

Why not buy another property as your equity grows over time, or diversify into high-yielding shares, or even buy a property using your superannuation fund. It's all very achievable.

The main outtake, though, is simple:

Do *something*. *Never* do nothing.

There's just one word of warning. Always allow for affordability in your strategy. For example, if interest rates move higher, so too will your loan repayments. Fortunately, if interest rates rise, so does inflation and rent, unless things get ugly and go the other way. Of course, then we'd all be in trouble but at least interest rates will be low, making affordability easier. As a rule of thumb, allow for 2% to 3% above the current interest rate and try to build in some equity to cover you during periods of vacancy, or when you're facing major repairs.

The key is to keep your living costs down, and that may be best achieved by actually buying a house. If you're over fifty, though, I will generally strongly recommend you consider interest-only payments and salary sacrificing the extra amount into a *safe* superannuation option, then paying out the balance of the loan tax-free when you reach sixty and retire. The passage of time should inflate your property's value.

At forty it's a different proposition. You probably have twenty-five years left in the work force, which is plenty of time to reap the rewards from a longer-term approach.

Superannuation

Before I lose you at this point, given the recent performance of managed superannuation has been so abysmal, just hear me out for a moment while I discuss a few do-it-yourself super options and the tax concessions that come with them, which simply *cannot* be ignored.

Tax-effective investment doesn't get any better than pre-tax contributions to superannuation.

Remember: superannuation contributions are taxed at a low 15%.

Compare this to the 34% tax rate most taxpayers face, and for every $100 you salary sacrifice into superannuation, you have an immediate saving of $19.00 in tax.[13]

13 The tax saving rises to $31.50 for a tax payer in the top tax bracket for 2013.

Simply by putting money into superannuation you have made an immediate 19% return on your pre-tax money (or the equivalent at the time of writing of around four years of term deposit interest).

Don't ignore the power of using *safe* superannuation for an effective post-divorce financial recovery.

Let's look at another example.

> *You're paying tax at the 34% tax rate and receive a $10,000 bonus. Ordinarily, you lose $3,400 in tax. Alternatively, if you declare prior to receiving your bonuses that it's to be paid directly into superannuation, you lose only $1,500 in tax. That's $1,900 that you get to keep.*
>
> *The catch, of course, is that you can't get to this money until you're old enough to retire.*
>
> *With superannuation, though, tax-effective savings don't stop at the contributions level, as earnings derived from superannuation are taxed at 10% to 15%. And after you've retired, it gets even better, as the earnings and payments out of the fund in most cases attract the almost unbelievable tax rate of zero percent (and yes, you read that right)!*

Another point to remember is that superannuation earnings aren't counted as income when it comes to child maintenance, which is something to consider (if appropriate) and discuss with your advisor. You may be better off putting your lump-sum divorce payout into *safe* super, especially if you're close to retiring.

A general rule with contributions to superannuation, though, is that before making additional salary sacrifice contributions, you should repay all your non-deductible loans (like home loans and credit cards) and expenses prior to reaching fifty. Once you've hit fifty, you consolidate and hold debt, and then it's all super contributions from that point on in nearly every case.

Remember, though, that until 2014 (at this stage), no matter what your age, the maximum deductible contribution you can make in a year falls to $25,000, so getting as close to that sum as possible each year over a longer period of time now becomes an even more critical priority.

Self-managed superannuation for dads

As a tax advisor, I see a lot of resistance to the idea of contributing more than legally required to superannuation. This is because many people don't like managed superannuation funds (usually due to fee structures, poor performance, and the ongoing fees paid to financial planners). For these people, running a self-managed superannuation fund (SMSF) is often the answer.

Sometimes it can be difficult to show the tax benefits from having $200,000 or more in a commercial fund. In these cases, it is often much easier to show the tax savings using an alternative: investing $200,000 or more into their own SMSF, which then buys a small factory (for example) and then rents it back to either the investor's business or someone else's. (And it's the same strategy for residential property, except you can't rent it back to yourself or an associate).

And from September 2007's clarification, SMSFs provide investors with the ability to make their own investment decisions, and to borrow through the prudent use of easily constructed instalment warrants, which is a form of derivative (and I often find myself advising clients about their benefits, not to mention doing a doctoral thesis on the topic and levels of measurement for safely-leveraged investment).

Let's look at some other examples.

You put $200,000 into your own SMSF, which then borrows a further $200,000 through an instalment trust structure and buys a factory that your SMSF rents back to either your (the superannuant's) business[14] or someone else's. A positive cash flow and your 9% payroll contributions plus any additional salary sacrifice can all help to pay down the loan very quickly indeed.

Your SMSF buys farming land and rents it back to you. You plant a tree plantation on it, claiming the tax deductions to do so (other tax deductions include annual expenses like the rent you're paying to your superannuation fund, insurance, plantation and financing costs) while your plantation grows till you reap the rewards of the harvest. As mentioned, your own superannuation fund can borrow through an instalment warrant to buy the land.

It sounds almost too good to be true, but it really is tax-effective reality!

Divorced mums

Divorced mums face a unique set of circumstances, and this section has been written specifically for them and the challenges they face.

Let's look at a common scenario and some of the mistakes that a typical divorced mum often makes. Let's say the mum receives 65% of the asset base, which often includes the family home (worth $500,000) and mortgage (say $200,000).

The mum often receives tax-free child maintenance and mostly

14 Remember that the arrangement in this case must be a commercially realistic one that will stand up to scrutiny, and not some dollar-a-month-type scam.

tax-free Centrelink benefits along with part-time work (in some cases) to live on and support the mortgage payments that came with the home.

Let's say our mum looks at the $200,000 mortgage she has inherited and decides to sell and buy a cheaper home for $350,000.

In the process, she has just lost $50,000 in stamp duty, agent's selling fees, advertising, moving costs, connection costs, etc, so she has decreased the mortgage by only $100,000 and now has a lower value asset that increases in value over time at a proportionally lower rate.

She has usually forgone the superannuation (in the settlement) or has a token amount of say $10,000 in an account that is being rapidly eroded by fees. Invariably, this amount is 'out of sight, out of mind'.

You might be surprised, but this example is a very common outcome. As with our divorcing dads, any divorce lawyer who doesn't instruct his or her client to seek separate financial advice and to have a plan for post-settlement recovery in place *before* accepting a settlement, needs to think hard about the service they're offering.

How to move on

To start the process of recovering, the most productive and empowering approach you can take is to pick up the pieces that remain and make a new start. Seize some sort of security. You're not alone. Make an appointment to see someone like myself, get some direction and get going again.

In this section, I'm going to talk about three possible roads to recovery (although irrespective of these strategies, I would also be urging any client of mine to consider a raft of other tax-effective investing strategies, regardless of their age or circumstances):

1. Keep the family home (or buy a home) using the bulk of the settlement.
2. Tax-effective investing (shares, rental property, etc) when you return to full-time work.
3. Review your superannuation and treat it seriously.

Don't sell the house!

When marriages break down and there are children involved, it's usually the dad who moves out, leaving mum to retain the family home.

Now, let's consider the example from the introduction, where the mum decides to sell and buy a cheaper home for $350,000. In the process, she has just lost $50,000 in selling and buying costs, so she has decreased the mortgage by only $100,000 and now has a lower value asset.

Even worse examples include instances where the mum sells the family home and places the sale proceeds in the bank.

Here's what's wrong with this situation:

- She loses an asset that will likely grow in value, importantly in untaxed dollars.
- The money received from the sale sits in a bank earning interest, which is taxed.
- The earnings from the sale proceeds effectively reduce pension entitlements, child maintenance, and other benefit entitlements, which are untaxed.
- And to top it all off, she's now paying rent in *after-tax* dollars. Mostly, it's all bad.

Now, I'm not saying the right strategy in every case involves hanging onto the family home, but in a lot of cases it is the very best way forward, and the numbers should always be crunched.

Tax usually isn't a problem for the divorced mum. Most of their 'income', including child maintenance (and in some cases spousal maintenance), part-time employment, untaxed (mostly) government benefits and other concessional rebates free a divorced mum of any significant tax obligation, so let's keep it that way.

If you feel you can't afford to hold onto the family home (or acquire one, which is equally as important), then there are two alternative strategies we can look at.

The first strategy involves moving from principal and interest mortgage repayments to paying interest only. Why would you do that? As they say, rent money is normally dead money (with some exceptions), and you don't have any claim on the appreciating value of property that's not yours. So why not pay a similar or lesser amount to enjoy both the security of owning your own home as well as the likely capital appreciation over time?

For example, if you have a $200,000 mortgage at 6.00%, you only need to pay around $231 or less per week in interest, which is usually much cheaper than rent!

The second strategy is based on the notion that in the short term it's better to watch a loan go up and win in the long term on tax-free capital growth. For example, consider a $400,000 mortgage (on a $600,000 home) at 6% requiring approximately $461 per week in repayments. Let's say we can only afford $400 per week. Remember from earlier that it costs upwards of $50,000 to sell and buy again at these levels. Let's (conservatively) assume a 5% growth rate of $30,000 per annum compounding and equivalent rent of $400. It's not hard to do the numbers, is it? To save $61 per week (a little more than $3,000 a year) we're losing $30,000 a year in tax–free, compounding asset appreciation.

At this point, we also need to review our other credit facilities and consolidate expensive debt (credit cards, leases, etc), which are all paid in after-tax dollars. Just don't borrow like this anymore. Draw a line in the sand and make the change.

If there is no home, then look at buying one as soon as possible with the proceeds of your divorce settlement. After the global financial crisis, credit is a lot harder to get, but there are still ways that require a lateral-thinking approach. For example, negotiate to keep the ex' on the loan if you've kept the home, or look to family or friends to help get you re-started.

Investing – can you afford it?

If you're under fifty and have returned to work full time, then you're probably ready to consider a raft of different investment options (and if not, then the reality is that the children are probably taking up way too much of your time, income and effort).

In most cases, however, and where income and equity allows, you should consider investing tax-effectively in another property or shares or any one of a number of other asset classes.

Consider again our previous example to illustrate the point, where we borrowed $400,000 for a house/unit for a total cash flow loss of only $1,560. It's a minor cash flow loss at worst, and for a conservative capital growth rate of 5%, equating to $20,000 per year, every year.

It really is a terrific scenario if you can manage it.

Superannuation for mums over fifty

I've already mentioned that superannuation contributions are taxed at a low 15%, and when compared to the 34% tax rate most taxpayers face, that for every $100 you salary sacrifice into superannuation, you have an immediate saving of $19.00 in tax[15] (providing an immediate 19% return on your pre-tax money, or the equivalent at the time of writing of around four years of term deposit interest). The power of using *safe* superannuation for an effective post-divorce financial recovery is undeniable.

Let's look at an example.

> *You're offered a new job that gives you a salary increase of $10,000 and you pay tax at the 34% tax rate. Normally, you'd lose $3,400 in tax on this pay increase and be left with just $6,600. Alternatively, if you salary sacrifice the pay boost into superannuation, you lose only $1,500 in tax. That's $1,900 you now get to keep. Don't forget the catch, of course: you can't get to this money until retirement.*
>
> *With superannuation, though, the tax-effective savings don't stop at the contributions level, as earnings derived from superannuation funds are taxed at 10% to 15%. And don't forget that after you've retired it gets even better, as the earnings and payments out of the fund don't get taxed at all!*

As a general rule with superannuation, don't forget that if you're under fifty, before making additional contributions, look at repaying all your non-deductible loans and other expenses.

Self-managed superannuation for mums

It can be difficult to show the tax benefits from putting money into

15 The tax saving rises to $31.50 for a tax payer in the top tax bracket for 2013.

managed superannuation funds, and especially so when it comes to divorced mums. And just like divorced dads, it's a lot easier to demonstrate the tax savings with an alternative.

So let's do that now:

> *Let's say you invest $300,000 (additional cash or with no home, the example is the same) in your own SMSF, which then buys a house in an area that you want to move to when you retire (on the coast, for example). In the meantime you rent it out, with the rental income flowing to your SMSF.*
>
> *Not only is this a good strategy from the point of view that it effectively provides you with another (or possibly your only) capital gains tax-exempt property when you take it as a lump sum once you've reached sixty (or retired), the rental income to your SMSF is also taxed at only 15%.*

SMSFs also provide investors with the ability to make their own investment decisions. And as I've already mentioned, SMSFs are able to borrow funds, especially since the ATO's September 2007 clarification, via the prudent use of easily constructed instalment warrants.

Let's look at some examples of how that can work for divorced mums.

> *You put $250,000 into your SMSF, which then borrows a further $150,000 through an instalment trust structure to buy a shop front, which the SMSF then rents back to either your business or someone else's. Already highly cash-flow positive, with your 9% payroll contributions, any additional salary sacrifice contributions will only help pay down the loan even faster.*
>
> *Your SMSF uses half its funds to buy a share portfolio or a simpler, diversified index fund that's yielding 6% (with tax*

credits), and places the other half of its funds in term deposits yielding 5%. The yields from both already provide a great income stream in retirement, but the 50% held in cash can also be used to draw down on when needed, particularly during years of poor share market performance, enabling you to wait out an eventual recovery while leaving the capital balance intact.

Divorced soloists

A soloist is really anyone who doesn't have dependent children, and a divorced soloist should be self-explanatory. Soloists face an entirely different set of circumstances to divorced mums and dads. The main issue for this group is re-establishing independence while returning to a single income, and dealing with all the additional costs that come with once again being on your own.

Let's look at a common scenario and some of the mistakes that a soloist often makes.

A soloist couple divorces. One half receives 50% of the asset base, which normally includes a residence (say $500,000) and a mortgage (say $200,000), while the other typically receives cash or other assets in settlement.

Let's assume the soloist with the $200,000 mortgage decides to sell and buy a cheaper house or unit for $350,000. Automatically, they have just lost $50,000 in stamp duty, agent's selling fees, advertising, moving costs, etc, while only reducing their mortgage by $100,000, leaving them with an asset of lower value that increases at a proportionally lower rate.

For soloists, though, the outcome is often far worse than this, given they generally feel less restrained when it comes to entering new relationships. They meet someone more quickly, re-partner

> *more quickly, and then end up selling the property they just dropped $50,000 on to once again buy and move into a new area . . .*

You might be surprised, but this example represents a disturbingly common outcome. And once again, any divorce lawyer who doesn't instruct his or her client to seek separate financial advice and to have a plan in place for their post-settlement recovery *before* accepting a settlement should be wracked with guilt.

How to move on

The most productive and empowering approach anyone can take to starting the recovery process is to pick up the pieces and make a new start. Remember, you're not alone. Make an appointment to see a financial adviser, get some direction, and get going again.

1. Aim to keep the home or unit if the settlement has granted it to you (as with the divorced mum's scenario). If not, look at buying a new home, especially if you're under fifty (as with the divorced dad's scenario).
2. Review your superannuation and start taking it seriously, but in most cases don't contribute more than what's legally required until you reach fifty.
3. Once life has calmed down a little, look at some tax-effective investing (buying a rental property, shares, etc). Establishing yourself on one income will take time to adjust to, so think of this as part of your longer-term plan.

Hold onto (or get hold of) a house

More often than not, the soloist faces a situation where downsizing a property looks to be the most appropriate or even the only possible decision, because there's only one income now to support it.

Remember, though, that your first priority should always be holding onto a home (even if it's just for the transactional cost savings), and if you cannot afford to stay or choose not to, then rent a place somewhere else. My key point in these cases is that this is often the best way forward.

If you really think you can't afford to hold onto the home (or acquire one, which is equally as important) then there are two strategies we can look at to assist with holding or acquiring.

One involves moving from principal and interest mortgage repayments to paying interest only, and the other is based on the notion that it's better in the short term to watch a loan go up (capitalise) and win in the long term with tax-free capital growth.

Reread the section for divorced mums for a detailed rationale.

Why is this all so important?

There are two reasons.

Firstly, owning a property is important because it builds wealth no matter how small the base, and wealth gives you choices (which become especially important when you're on your own). For example, if you fall sick and you need to stop working, having an asset to fall back on allows you to do this more comfortably than if you have nothing at all.

Secondly, banks love equity and will readily lend against it, affording you wealth-building opportunities along the way, which leads us into the next stages in the soloist's financial recovery.

Invest tax-effectively

Once your life has been consolidated and you have your finances sorted and under some sort of control (and you are still under the age of fifty), you're ready to consider a raft of options.

In most cases, and where income and equity allows, you should consider investing tax-effectively into another property or shares or any one of a number of other asset classes. There are plenty to choose from and most are cost-neutral at the moment (meaning there are no out-of-pocket expenses).

Let's look at a variation on our previous property investment example, but with an entirely different asset base.

Loan for a balanced share portfolio	$400,000
Interest payable at 6%	($24,000)
Dividends received (including tax credits)	$24,000
Tax loss	**$0**
Cash flow loss	**$0**

So you break even. And if you consider even a conservative capital growth rate of 5%, this equates to $20,000 per annum compounding on your initial $400,000 investment.

Over time you're going ahead. The share dividend yields will inevitably increase, the debt will slowly be repaid, the gap between annual growth of $20,000 and your net expenses grows, and so does your ability to invest again.

On a personal note, over time I do not believe a diversified portfolio is any riskier than owning a property when we're talking about blue-chip stocks, but I do understand I'm in the minority in holding this view. There is no doubt that shares are more volatile, but then property can be volatile, too. Try selling a house or a commercial property in a generally falling property market!

Just as the case with property, in the short term, even when the market is volatile, *don't* sell your blue-chip shares (or for that matter even so much as *look* at their values).

Superannuation for soloists

When it comes to superannuation, the lessons learned from examining some of the strategies for divorced dads and mums apply every bit as much to the soloist. And by now we should really be grasping the fact that tax-effective investment doesn't get any better than when we're making *pre-tax* contributions to our superannuation.

Taxed at only 15% before you retire, and then not at all once you retire (and it can't ever get better than 0%), compare this to the 34% tax rate most taxpayers face. You're getting a 19% return by simply putting extra pre-tax money into superannuation, or a 31.5% return if you're in the top tax bracket.

Remember the general rule, though, when considering extra contributions to superannuation. If you're younger than fifty, repay all your non-deductible loans and other expenses first. And don't forget that until 2014 (at the time of writing), the maximum contribution you can make in a year falls to $25,000, so getting as close to that sum as possible each year over a longer period of time has become an even greater priority.

Self-managed superannuation for soloists

I won't repeat what I've already said about the resistance I often encounter to making extra contributions to superannuation, or the solution a SMSF can often provide, because it's no different when it comes to soloists. So let's look at another brief example of a strategy we can employ with a SMSF.

> *Consider the case where $400,000 is being held in a commercial fund that has lost another $100,000 in the latest financial year alone. In these cases, it is much easier to show the*

tax savings with an alternative, such as investing the $400,000 in an SMSF, which then buys a diversified share portfolio along with a rolling hedging strategy to avoid further losses.

Let's say this $400,000 was invested in a SMSF, which then borrows a further $250,000 through an instalment trust structure, buys a block of land in rural Australia for $350,000, and then leases the land out for agistment or for crops.

The remaining $300,000 can then be used to purchase $150,000 worth of diversified shares and $150,000 can be placed into term deposits or bonds with part of the yields of both contributing to a hedging strategy for the exposed $150,000 share portfolio.

SUMMING IT ALL UP

There are numerous strategies covered in this chapter and throughout the entire book that will substantially enhance a financial recovery, and more importantly overcome one of the most debilitating financial distractions there is: *divorce.*

Let's just sum up what you need to do:

- Get advice and get it quickly (prior to settlement).
- When under fifty, try to keep or buy a home.
- Invest tax-effectively when the timing is appropriate.
- Maximise the super power of superannuation, especially for the over fifties.

Superannuation's power includes:

- Immediate tax-effective returns on your contributions.
- Concessional (low) tax rates on earnings.
- Tax-free status at age fifty-five/sixty (and semi-retired/retired).
- The ability to borrow through instalment warrants (enabling your SMSF to borrow to buy property).

CHAPTER ELEVEN

SELF-EMPLOYMENT

Financial distraction and self employment go hand-in-hand, which is why this chapter is the *second* biggest in the book. From my experience, most of the financial distraction that comes from self-employment stems from the simple imperative every self-employed person faces: grow, grow, and grow (and all things growth).

Sometimes growth is desirable and very much to be sought after, and sometimes it comes whether you want it to or not. With constant growth, however, comes a steady stream of financial distractions that need to be managed.

I work with small to medium-sized businesses on a daily basis. This has enabled me to observe this phenomenon in very close quarters over at least the last sixteen years, and this chapter addresses the issues with growth that I've seen first hand.

Growth can be the most distracting of all the financial distractions, which makes it extremely important to learn how to go with growth rather than fighting it, how to understand it, and how to begin the process of eliminating the financial distractions that growth can bring.

A common perception is that with growth comes freedom, which may be true eventually (if you get there), but before this can happen there will be the inevitable cycles of negative cash flow, lending issues and debtor defaults, all of which grow as well, along with increasing income taxes, GST liabilities, payroll taxes, staff and union agreements (but I'd better stop this list here as this chapter is actually intended to encourage growth, not put you off).

Manufacturing in Australia is dying and retailing is taking a battering, and this situation will only get worse. It seems that services are the last bastion of the potentially decent return for effort, unless you want to be a miner (and remember that eventually all resource cycles turn down, too).

If you're in manufacturing or retail though, then you really must at least look at adding a service to compliment your activities if you want to survive, and this chapter is intended to provide you with a few ideas to consider.

This chapter focuses on the service industry. Services come in all shapes and sizes, from plumbers, truck drivers, and accountants, to lawyers, fitness trainers, cooks and musicians. Name anything that uses a human to serve something in some way shape or form, and you're talking about a service.

A retailer and a manufacturer must add a service to succeed as the world gets smaller, digitized and even more competitive than before, so let's address these two sectors first.

Retailers

There are many different ways a retailer can add services to their business model. For example, a shoe store might bring in shoe fitting or an in-house podiatrist, a clothing store may offer in-house tailors, or a pool shop can also offer water testing along with a pool cleaning service. A great example involves an electrical retailer who, while his competitors complained about internet sales destroying their businesses, started a service to deliver and install the electronic equipment he was selling.

Other examples include the piano shop that starts a piano courier franchise, the music store that provides affordable in-house music lessons, the auto store that fits your windscreen wiper blades, or the small hardware store that organises trades services (they probably know all the local tradesmen anyway), which also encourages those same tradesmen to buy from the store.

Store credit, after-sales service and information about new products are all services that are usually offered, but need to be expanded on. Provide a service and retail sales will soon follow, and when you put your mind to it you can always think of a service to add to retail beyond just providing exceptional customer service (which is essential).

The reality is that without that extra element of service, you're going to be in real trouble (but I suspect no one in retailing today needs me to tell them that). My thinking here is to simply make a change in yours: think of your retail store as a loss leader to direct business into the more profitable area of service provision. It's a great opportunity, so why not embrace it?

Manufacturers

For manufacturing, life has well and truly changed. It's no longer about quoting on a job and manufacturing to a specification. That kind of competitive edge is long gone.

In today's environment, a manufacturer's survival depends on adaptability and working niches that target smaller volumes with bigger margins, because anything that can be produced in volume will be produced in countries with lower labour costs.

The answer is to think laterally and target products that make things easier for their consumers. For example, heavy products are becoming expensive to install due to increasingly stringent workplace health and safety laws, and long gone are the days when one man will carry forty or more kilograms (and cement bags are smaller these days for that very reason).

Cranes, scaffolds, hoists and various other types of heavy lifting equipment are the obvious response, incurring significant extra costs. So why not consider making plastic chattel and product alternatives that are just as strong, significantly lighter, look great, and are cheaper to produce?

The pool market provides yet another example, where you can expect to pay $100,000 or more for a concrete pool with all the bells and whistles, while the plastic alternatives are currently nothing short of tragic.

Alternatively, make a high quality product that targets the do-it-yourself market, and away you go.

Any area where technical skills are important also offers great potential margins, but you have to be the innovator. Look for technical skills and needs, and manufacture to improve on the way things are done.

It's my belief that not only changing labour laws and practices represent the greatest opportunities in all fields (construction, mining, retail, services etc), but also that bringing a technical skill set to manufacturing is essential. You can't be a follower. You need to be a leader. So get thinking and get doing.

Business growth

Just as in life, a business will wither and die if it doesn't grow. There are different ways to achieve growth, however, that can offer a new solution to the problems growth can create by combining the benefits of a bigger business with the magical benefits of a boutique business.

A boutique business occupies a profitable niche, and in a profitable niche there is generally little scope for expansion, as the business normally hinges on you and so is at risk of falling away if there's no growth.

Let's say you've built up a successful, service-based business or have now added a successful service base to your retail and manufacturing business.

Your first problem is that the business now revolves around you, which is normally the case when you've established a successful service-based element, as the service has to have come from you.

Your second problem, though, is that it can't be as successfully delegated to anyone else because it needs the passion and the technical drive only you, its owner and creator, can provide. And you've done this by providing great customer service and technical skill, as well as going that extra yard to help your customers because you had the time, drive and the obvious ability to do so.

Now you're overloaded (distracted) and you have a choice to make. Do you get bigger or go boutique (specialise), or do you do nothing at all and just learn to love the stress?

As your service business grew, your customers loved the service you offered and referred you to others (and we all like the income and capital growth that new customers can bring). The problems only begin to emerge, however, when you reach your saturation point. You're simply too busy to provide the service you used to provide, and dissatisfaction sets in: personal dissatisfaction, because being overloaded means you aren't really enjoying the business anymore, and customer dissatisfaction, because you aren't providing the same level of service they're used to.

This all spells major distraction.

The decision to move to a boutique operation or bigger business can be as simple as a lifestyle choice (pulling back) or a success choice (building a big business). Whatever your motivation, though, this chapter explores both paths, while finally offering a third alternative, which is a mixture of the two.

Not making a decision, however, is probably the worst thing you can do, and merely means more of the same and no end to your financial distractions.

So let's examine your choices.

The river

Right now you're too busy to provide the service standard you used to provide. So imagine that at this moment in time you're standing on the bank of a river.

> *On the other side is your bigger business. To get there, though, you have to cross a fierce-looking torrent. In addition, even if you think you've found an easier point to cross at (one that may appear relatively calm) you still need to beware. There may still be strong under-currents that can catch you out.*
>
> *This river is also full of hidden dangers that can quickly pull you off your feet: capital requirements, staff, work-cover costs, payroll tax, superannuation, time, financial hardship, the risk of losing it all, a lack of resources, and the list goes on.*
>
> *The dangers seem almost endless.*

All of these challenges must be met if you're going to reach the side where your successful bigger business resides.

The alternative, of course, is to stay where you are, to not cross the river, and remain a small business. However, you and your customers will never be satisfied if you do. As your service levels start to drop, customer tension and dissatisfaction will increase and your customers will begin to leave, but you continue to generate new customers (in what I call the 'vicious time-wasting circle', which I'll discuss in a moment).

In the worst case, you lose more customers than you gain and the business that you have worked so hard to build starts to decline. But maybe this isn't the worst case. Maybe the worst case is that you actually manage to receive more referrals than losses, which will increase the dissatisfaction felt by both you and your customers.

Now let's look a little more closely at the vicious time-wasting circle.

The vicious time-wasting circle

Think of the amount of time you spend bringing a new customer on board, and the advertising costs, set-up costs, administration costs, and relationship building that are required to do so. In reality, it's much easier to keep and maintain customers you've already built a relationship with, rather than to keep on chasing new ones to replace the customers you're losing.

In a service-based business, proactivity is a major tool for maintaining and building your business from within. Sadly, customer dissatisfaction and loss is a symptom of the exact opposite.

But back to our metaphor.

Before you reached the river, whenever you looked at your list of customers (your database), you always spotted opportunity, served your customers well, and provided ideas and solutions. You felt satisfied and your customers did, too. Now you're too busy, you're not looking to your database for opportunities, and you're struggling to find the time to service the customers you have, let alone actively look for new opportunities. Your customers trust you, want to be served by you, and are willing to listen to your ideas and solutions. They rely on you for this proactivity. The problem is that you're not providing it because you're just too busy.

You're letting your customers down.

And because of this, you're at grave risk of falling into the vicious time-wasting circle.

The fact is, when you're truly standing at the river's edge, you're ignoring the best resource you have, which is your database. By using your database, you avoid the added dollar costs required to bring in new customers, not to mention the extra time and cost required to establish new relationships.

It's a simple principal. If you don't serve your customers you'll lose them. Whether you choose to build a big business or go boutique, before you spend money or time on external growth opportunities, you should look inwards first. Remember, your customers want proactivity and will seek it elsewhere if you don't supply it.

It's a common cycle, really, one I have observed on many occasions. A new business will come along, chasing market share (in the growth stage and well before reaching the riverbank), offering the type of service that you used to offer. Before you know it, you've lost a customer.

Now we've had a good look at what confronts us, let's look at crossing the 'river' and growing our business. And to do this, we need to examine the most common alternatives to survive the torrent and get across to the other side.

Business growth

The best way to grow a business is to simplify and systemise. Most businesses can be systemised, and if anyone you know claims their industry's peculiarities mean this can't be done, they're either wrong or just too busy to see the wood for the trees.

All businesses, to varying degrees, can be systemised.

What people fail to understand is that when you're standing on the river bank, you're in the perfect position to systemise. Your customers understand the need for change. In fact, they're probably already starting to get tired of your excuses and will tolerate the adjustment. The most vital aspect is that you improve your service in this transition period. If you don't, your customers will soon lose patience. To prevent this, show them the benefits of change and show it to them quickly.

Generally, business success comes in one of three ways.

> *"... Luck... ", when someone falls into the right opportunity at the right time and success comes naturally.*
>
> *"... Capital... ", by throwing capital at a project and employing the best, with no costs spared.*
>
> *"... Hard work... ", through sheer hard work and determination, which is the lot most of us are stuck with, unless we're lucky enough to have capital dripping from our fingers.*

This chapter's focus involves the route requiring sheer hard work and determination, because it's clearly the most distracting. It concentrates on small service businesses facing growth challenges arising from building a service business from scratch or adding services to retail and manufacturing, with minimal equity and little luck.

The most important component of growing a business is planning. Business planning makes things happen. A lack of planning leads to wondering what went wrong. Without a structured plan in place, the chances of success are slim, especially in a competitive, service-based marketplace. There are a myriad of business books (notably, Gerber's 'E-myth' series), consultants, courses and advisors around to help cross this river, but it also takes real commitment, capital, compromise, and courage.

Staffing

One of the biggest issues in building a service-based business is staff. In a service-based industry, having effective staff is the key. Using the same principal as product in the manufacturing industry, the importance of staff in service-based business growth cannot be overstated. The problem is that it's almost impossible (I believe) over the long term to get employees who will provide the same level of service as you, and simply because it's not their business and they don't care as much.

When staff are diligent enough to care, then they'll often appreciate the money and the opportunities you've created, and will want to be self-employed themselves, ending up competing against you, or even taking your customers with them.

Staff leave for a myriad of reasons: health, family, babies, better offers, interstate moves, personality clashes, travel, and the list goes on. No matter the reason, exiting staff are a reality that must be considered, even if you're a fantastic boss and pay excellent wages.

However, by simplifying and systemising staff roles (like McDonald's™ does in the food industry) you take control of this key resource. Training and developing staff becomes easier and the threat from them leaving, and you having to replace them, is significantly diminished. Likewise, the reliance the customer has on that staff member is transferred to a reliance on the business. The result is that if a key staff member leaves, the customer doesn't go with them.

Delegation

Delegation is another important consideration. Remember, in a service-based industry, the customer likes to deal with you. You offer the best service and they don't want to deal with your juniors. However, customers also accept and understand that you can't do everything, and will accept this situation as long as you're still the communication point and take responsibility for your juniors.

For example, let's say you clean one office at 5:00 PM each night of the week. Because you do such a great job, one of your customers refers you to one of their business associates. Now you have six offices to be cleaned at 5:00 PM over a five-day week, and need to employ someone to help. If you employ someone and send them to do the job, the level of service may not be as good as what you're offering now, and for the reasons I mentioned earlier. Alternatively, if it is, your new employee may soon tire of receiving $25 an hour, especially when they know you're getting $55 an hour, and may decide to undercut you at $40 an hour.

Everyone wins except you. All the time spent winning the customer, setting them up administratively, building a relationship and training the staff member, has been for nothing.

In this situation, the solution is still to employ someone, but rotate them between workplaces. Turn up at the job with them and make contact with the customer (so the customer still knows he's dealing with you). In other words, once a month or so, someone else cleans each customer's workplace, but three times a month the customer is served by you.

Continue this procedure right up until you're personally cleaning once a month or not at all. Rotate the staff and personally visit your customers at the start of jobs even if it's only once a month (this way the customer still knows they're dealing with you). Be the main phone contact and, above all, ensure the customer is fully served.

Growing a business is a decision. Once you make the decision, you're fully committed to the whole process. You can't be half-hearted, as you'll surely tire of fighting the current and turn around and head back to the riverbank. Don't let this chapter discourage you from taking the challenge, though. The aim here is simply to highlight some of the challenges and offer some alternatives.

How growth affects profit

Let's take a look at how all this growth impacts on profits, on the basis of hours worked by the principal 'server' for a given return.

Profit, as a percentage of principal hours actually worked, will dip with growth. The main reason for this is simple. You're accepting all types of work, including the profitable, the not-so-profitable, and the work where you may just break even or even make a loss. The thing is your profits will be higher on a percentage-of-hours-worked basis if you simply take the good work and forget the bad.

The case for a boutique business, which I'll present shortly, focuses on only accepting the good work, and letting go of or changing the way you do the bad work to make room for more of the good (unless all your work is good, in which case you're in an excellent position to choose either path).

Other reasons that contribute to the profit dip generally focus on one staff member offering poor service, rushed jobs, rework, etc. These are costs. For example, let's say you have an apprentice you charge out at $55 per hour and pay $15 per hour. However, every fifth job requires re-work. This costs you time in customer service, time to go back and repair, and the time the apprentice spent (poorly) in the first place. It's another vicious time-wasting circle.

Remember, that as the key service provider, you're worth more than $55 per hour. The work you do, whether generating more work or higher-charged work, cannot now be done because you're fixing/organising other work. Magnify this by 10 apprentices and you have no time left.

The key is you need to remember the value of your time and the hours you work and to learn how to maximise it. When you do this, the profits will follow, but initially it takes time.

Standing on the riverbank

Now back to our metaphor for a moment.

> *You hit the riverbank. Crossing means you'll need to dedicate more hours to the business and, as a percentage, the profit return on those hours will fall. However, if you stick at it and commit even more hours, returning less overall, then eventually, if the business succeeds, a better percentage return on your investment is the result.*

The worst thing you can do at this point is to cross only half way, then turn back simply because the water was too cold or the current running too fast. I've seen it many times. People head into the river with hopes of crossing it, only to discover mid way that their income is dropping, taxes and on-costs are increasing, and finance is running out. Then they retreat.

This is probably the worst result possible, as all the money, time, and effort have been wasted. The worst part is that even when a business retreats, in time the cycle will only emerge again.

Boutique

It's time now to look at the boutique route as an alternative to developing a big business. This differs from the development cycle I've been talking about so far. Instead of a drop in profit for every hour worked, profit remains the same, and if things are done correctly, should increase, but rarely to the lofty heights that a successful big business generates. That's the trade off.

Using our 'river' metaphor, the boutique alternative means you don't cross the river. Instead, you walk along the bank until you find an estuary, and then find yourself a niche.

When I say niche, or use the word 'boutique', neither has to be in the truest sense of these words, or even in the form of a different service to the one you're offering now. It means doing what you're doing now, but doing it much better than anyone else, or focusing on a certain type of customer or service you offer. This may mean sacking bad customers and spending more time on your good ones.

Remember, bad customers consume too much of your time, but worse still, bad customers generally refer other bad customers to you. It's a must to break this cycle before it starts to consume your database.

Sometimes we need to free up some time to build the boutique business. In terms of things that may affect this by being a waste of time, here are some of my pet hates.

Travel

How many hours a day do you lose travelling? Some service industries obviously need to travel, like industrial cleaning and electrical work, but many service industries can save money by not travelling, and instead using couriers to deliver or pick up items for repair, delivering goods to sites, etc. Stick to your local area, or learn the value of a courier. At around $10 to deliver across town same day, why would you do it yourself?

Alternatively, move your on-the-road service to an in-house service. I believe that perceptions are changing. Customers no longer mind travelling to see you, and are just as happy (if not happier) with contact via phone and email.

Where it was once the norm for service-providing professionals to do home visits, I actually don't think many people feel all that comfortable inviting you into their home/business anymore. The cost of a serviced office or a sub lease on an office is minimal and your productivity soars.

Quoting

Nearly everyone I meet in the service industry complains about how much time is wasted on quoting. My answer is 'avoid it'. Instead, give prices for products. For example, how much for a power point, replacement antenna installation, new hard drive in a computer, a standard office clean, an hourly rate, etc. Explain that the prices you give are for general work, and if you encounter any problems, you'll contact them, explain the difficulty, and advise them of the extra costs involved. In the overwhelming majority of cases, the customer will simply accept this and approve. If they don't, then move on (it will rarely happen). Communications skills are the key here.

For bigger jobs that do require a quote, work on building relationships so your quote can be informal, based on earned trust, and quick. Make sure you always err on the side of caution, and only raise issues above your quoted price if they really are unforeseeable.

Remember, your time is a valuable commodity, so waste as little as possible on quoting. Maybe even consider a quoting fee on jobs, where you feel you have little chance of winning or if you feel the customer is just playing you off against a competitor.

One customer

The worst thing you can do is to focus on only one customer, thereby putting all your eggs in one basket (with the potential to destroy the business, not to mention wasting the time spent in building it up). Spread your risk. That way, if one customer goes broke or uses someone else, you still survive.

I have seen this with clients who have a very successful business on paper, only to see it disappear when a major retail chain decides to buy elsewhere. Diversification is the key. If you're stuck with one or more major clients, then make sure you service them and stay at the head of your competitive market place, because someone is surely looking at you and your market share.

In the boutique, there is only one golden rule: service and quality of service. Raise your level of service and the referrals will flow, customer retention will be excellent, and the profits will increase.

Putting it simply, in business there are three factors: service, quality and price. You only need two factors to be profitable.

If you offer all three, then success is guaranteed.

Boutiques offer all three with a reduced focus on price. In addition, a key to running a profitable boutique involves reduced costs and minimal overheads. The result is that when you work it's all cream, and when you take on extra work or harvest extra work from your database, then it's cream and cream of the sweetest kind.

For example, imagine you're in the service-based business of tree lopping. You currently cut the trees down and mulch them, or take away the timber. So why not value add? You already have an existing customer and you're there on the spot. Instead of cutting the logs up for firewood and leaving them there for passers-by to pick up, why not take them with you. Why not establish a yard where you dry the wood and then split and sell it. Even better still, if the tree you've just cut down is of a good quality, why not establish relationships with saw millers, or mill it yourself in the yard you have for firewood, and sell it directly to woodworkers? In this yard you establish, you could also sell the mulch, instead of leaving it or getting rid of it cheaply, or even worse, having to pay for its disposal.

Strengths, Weaknesses, Opportunities, and Threats

Most of us know what a SWOT analysis is. Put simply, it's a review of the strengths, weaknesses, opportunities and threats facing a business. This long-standing, simple analytical approach can be used to find a starting point when adopting boutique-based business strategies, right through to monitoring and evaluating ongoing performance.

Regardless of where your business is in terms of the growth stage, it's important to continue to monitor your position. SWOT is simple and you should sit down (preferably with your advisor) and go through the analysis on a regular basis. It's surprising what it will throw up when you put aside the time.

One final suggestion is to sell products you consume in your service industry. That is, selling the consumables you use, but at a marked-up price. For example, imagine you're in the storage industry and consume vast amounts of storage boxes and storage systems. You have very good buying power with these products due to your consumption, so why not sell the consumable for a profit to people moving houses, or businesses using on-site storage, etc.

Is it that simple?

Is it that simple to either build your business fully committed, or take up an estuary and find a niche? Yes, it is. In the long run, though, the benefits flowing from a successful big business are usually greater than a boutique business. There's more money and, importantly, a greater capital value for the business. However, it's also important to remember that creating a big business is a long haul, and sacrifices have to be made. Don't undertake this type of growth unless you're fully committed. Plan it thoroughly, and the rewards are there if the business service is sound.

On the other hand, finding a niche offers lifestyle benefits, better profitability in the short to mid term, and a steady income over the long term. I'm finding more and more people are taking this 'sea-change' approach, and focusing more on lifestyle, parenthood, etc.

And this touches on another favourite topic of mine, which I talked about earlier on in the book, which is the concept of working flat out to achieve early retirement, verses later retirement with a focus on fewer business commitments.

Why retire at fifty-five?

One of the downsides of dealing with thousands of people a year is that some of them don't actually live that long, or their quality of life diminishes due to poor health.

So, why work hard to retire at fifty-five? Why not pace yourself and just work longer?

A theory I'm working on is to work forever, but reduce my time to three to four days a week before I reach fifty, and two to three days a week before sixty (and beyond). It's a plan that also avoids the need for having a large superannuation fund for retirement, but one that requires extensive planning, the reduction of debt and overheads, and a level of insurance cover for life, trauma and income-protection.

My only problem at present is that I still love my work and don't want to reduce my hours. But the time for more balance will eventually come.

Hybrid

Now I want to talk about yet another alternative, and that's the hybrid, and this involves mixing the two approaches I've just talked about.

It's possible to become big and yet remain a boutique business. One way is to bring in juniors/trainees/apprentices, and train them well. Once they get to the point where you can't economically pay them enough to keep them (meaning they may go out into the marketplace on their own), you then sell part of your business to them, or help establish them in business and keep the network you've already built.

This network is controlled by you (while it's also making a profit) through a service trust/administrative entity, so all parties receive the economies of scale for the costs (as do you) that a large business achieves, while keeping all your staff in the loop when they progress to the point of self-employment.

Imagine ten small businesses operating together in the same industry, combining their buying power to purchase materials, reducing costs to share administration expenses, covering for each other when the other needs a break, and providing the ability to work together on large jobs. An extension of the buying-group theme, there are many advantages to this approach.

The key here is to develop your staff. This way you keep a carrot in front of them (staff retention benefits). Be careful not to be greedy, though, by hanging onto them for too long. Think of the costs of losing some of your customers to them, employing and retraining someone else, and having to win new business simply to replace what you've lost.

For example, imagine a draftsperson who performs excellent work and who receives more and more referrals due to their quality of service. He is now at the banks of the river and makes the decision to hybridise by mixing big and boutique. To do this he employs two graduates straight from university who have the technical skills, but lack their employer's maturity and real-world experience. The wages he pays at this level are the base (cheap). The draftsperson now partly pulls back from the easier work, and develops systems so his graduates can easily understand his requirements and work with minimal supervision. This is the key. The systems must be simple and straightforward, and leave no room for his graduates to deviate.

This frees up the draftsperson to focus on his customer database, providing a proactive and fantastic service, which leads to more referrals. This also frees up the draftsperson to chase new work, both from his existing customers and from new customers entirely. The result is that the business continues to grow.

The hybrid deviation occurs three years down the track when the graduates are now making higher pay demands, are experienced, and can see the amount of money they too can make if they go out on their own. One is still happy to stay on as an employee for another couple of years, but the other is keen to move on.

The draftsman solves this dilemma by selling part of his database to the graduate wanting to leave, and sets up an administrative entity so he can stop paying a salary and they can begin to share costs: information technology costs, rental costs, photocopier costs, and various other business overheads. He then retains the customers he wants to keep, assists his graduate's career path, and retains the benefits of shared knowledge and the ability to cover for each other when on holiday, etc.

The business now suffers a drop in profitability due to a drop in fees, but makes savings on one graduate's wage, and through the economies of scale achieved from sharing overheads. This solution also frees the draftsman to pursue more work, either internally or externally, and the model grows and provides a capital return on their efforts.

SUMMING IT ALL UP

This chapter is not intended to be the be-all and end-all on this topic. Every single business and situation is different and there are other alternatives. The message here comes from my own experience in service-based businesses, and from working with clients in the service industry or retailers and manufacturers who are adding services to their business.

Solutions to whatever confronts you are out there, and I challenge anyone who says they can't do it to sit down with me and work through it. Changes can be made in every situation. The extent of that change is all that differs. It takes a lateral-thinking advisor to help your service-based business elements grow, someone who knows the service industry and can adapt his or her thinking to yours.

Financial distraction from self-employed growth has to be understood, put in context, and harnessed for a far greater good.

CHAPTER TWELVE

KEEPING KEY STAFF

This chapter should really be read by anyone who manages, leads, or employs people, but if you're a dissatisfied and distracted employee looking for lateral solutions to your career circumstances, then stick with it.

You need to read this chapter, too.

Financial distraction for employees

This chapter started life just prior to the onset of the global financial crisis (GFC), when the global economies were still booming. Employees were generally more ambitious when it came to wages and conditions, and weren't afraid of regularly switching jobs to improve both. This chapter springs from my advice to clients when it came to retaining their staff in that difficult environment.

Things have changed significantly since then, of course, and a lot of those employment pressures no longer exist, and mainly because people are more inclined to fear losing their job and not being able to find another one. It's also often the case that they are also confronting significantly increased levels of financial distraction since (and because of) the GFC.

Addressing financial distraction not only enhances an employee's engagement on the job (attention span, capacities at work, etc), but more importantly it also shows they're valued. And feeling valued at work often carries far greater significance to an employee than any salary package can offer, which fosters greater loyalty to the business.

Now for the burning question: how do we eliminate financial distraction for our employees?

We start by changing ourselves.

One of the greatest challenges a leader faces is learning to ensure distractions don't restrict their ability to effectively lead, and financial distraction is one of the biggest distractions any of us can face.

At the absolute core of financial distraction in the work place is the question of *why* we work (and if you've been reading from the start, then you'll be well versed on my response when it comes to this question).

It's obvious that personal financial circumstances will dictate your answer to the question of why you work, and affecting your work/life balance considerations, especially when you're financially existing day-to-day, with significant liabilities hanging over your head. Now compare this situation to someone who's been lucky enough to inherit (even significantly so).

Both these positions play a major part in any question concerning why we work (see Chapter 2 about work/life balance), and each can represent their own (although differing) levels of financial distraction. But don't think for a moment that someone with money is less financially distracted at work. This is a common misnomer. It's not necessarily financial circumstances that dictate a person's level of distraction, but rather the *attitude* to those circumstances.

So what are the major financial distractions for staff today? Almost too numerous to count, the main distractions involve debt, insufficient superannuation (and a loss of belief in superannuation altogether), salary package worth, the children's education costs, divorce, death, and chronic illness (and I deal with most of these throughout the book).

The point is that financial distraction is the same for nearly everyone, regardless of their position and no matter how large their income or assets.

So let's deal with these issues one by one.

Status-based financial distraction

Status and measures of worth are probably the most underrated financial distractions an employee faces. Fortunately, they're also among the easiest to address, so let's get this out of the way before we look at the process of eliminating actual financial distraction.

Simply put, status and measures of worth are financially distracting almost by definition, because people often view the amount they're paid as being a measure of both. The problem is that they'll often end up chasing money, and then more money, without actually getting what they really want, which is status and a measure of worth.

Sounds like a vicious circle without a solution, I know, but not when you understand that money is *not* the major contributing factor when it comes to status and measures of worth (as much as you may still be thinking it is).

So what's the answer? Well, it's actually very simple.

You tell them.

Communicate their status to them as well as to their colleagues, and by doing so show them how valuable they are. The result will be that the chase for money (financial distraction) will often very largely cease to be their primary focus. The reason why is equally as simple. We all want to feel important (and be *made* to feel important) no matter what our position is at work, and in reality an extra $10,000 a year in a pay packet really doesn't compare to the feeling of being vital to an organisation (and if it does, then the employee should probably be thinking about moving on anyway).

Working on both fronts—money-based financial distraction and status-based financial distraction—really represents working on the elimination of financial distraction within your organisation altogether. And in my experience, this two-pronged attack often brings almost immediate results in terms of increased employee engagement, improved productivity, and greater organisational motivation, loyalty and staff retention (not to mention reducing on-going recruitment and training costs).

Eliminating financial distraction is clearly a two-way street. By improving your staff's financial circumstances by eliminating financial distraction, you demonstrate an even greater value beyond the salary package.

We all appreciate being valued.

Money-based financial distraction

Speaking personally, I think one of the better ways to start this process of eliminating an employee's money-based financial distraction is by giving them a copy of this book. But not everyone learns from reading (or can be bothered), so a first step must generally come from a leader.

Listening is a great act of leadership (not to mention being a sign of respect), so start by sitting them down and really trying to understand their financial circumstances. I often work with a standard checklist (which you can find in Part 2 and How We Do It) that picks out the main financial distractions you need to address.

If you don't feel you're able to perform this role yourself, think about calling in a trusted advisor. You can even offer it as a free service to your employees.

Some of your people may be private types who find sharing information like this difficult. Generally, though, I find this is rare, especially with an independent advisor who can guarantee privacy and discretion when it comes to personal finances.

We all want to be a hero, and once you understand their financial circumstances it's your chance to be theirs.

So grab the chance and address the issues.

Let me show you a few examples of how:

> **Problem:** *a valued employee and mother to primary school-aged children is about to leave your employment, even though she loves her job and is truly excellent at it, because she's finding that before and after school child-care costs, combined with the loss of government benefits from being employed full time, are costing her more than she's earning. (If you haven't already, read my chapter on The Cost of Children for more about this particular financial distraction).*
>
> **Solution:** *in this case you're probably going to lose her no matter what, because it's senseless for her to stay. So retaining her in some capacity before she quits is likely to be a win. So try offering reduced hours, from say 9:30 AM to 3.00 PM, with a half-hour lunch break. She may even end up being more productive. Delegate the additional hours if you really need to (generally you won't). You get to keep a valuable employee and increase productivity, and as the children get older she may even be able to return to a full-time role.*

Problem: *a fifty-five year-old employee that you value has decided he only has ten more years left in the workforce, and his salary isn't high enough to meet his planned retirement saving needs. He's now told you he's quitting for a higher-paying job even though he loves working for you, and the new travel time will add an hour each day.*

Solution: *now he's reached fifty-five, he can start transitioning to a retirement pension, imaginatively named a Transition to Retirement pension, by applying to his superannuation fund. He then can put his Transition to Retirement pension payments back into super (because the income his superfund balance earns is now taxed at a significantly lower rate), along with some additional contributions of his own via salary-sacrificing.*

With some advice, he can also reconsider his level of risk in his superfund, for example by switching to blue-chip stocks or cash deposits, to give him the confidence to make extra contributions at this late stage without losing money.

Once the Transition to Retirement pension payments start, the income his superfund balance earns will stop being taxed altogether, so his fund value will grow even faster. Even better, when he reaches sixty, the pension payments he receives will be completely tax free, and he is able to re-contribute the larger, tax-free amounts, further accelerating the growth of his retirement funds. (If you're super interested in how the transition to retirement works, you can flip to my chapter on the Three Pillars for more about this particular strategy).

Problem: *your young superstar employee has decided it's time to strike out on their own, and is about to go into competition* *with you (see my chapter on Self-Employment), especially given they know you charge their services out at $75 per hour while paying them $35.*

Solution: *you have two solutions for two problems. The first problem is that you're losing a great colleague, and the second is that you're likely about to lose some good clients, as well. The solutions involve you either making them a partner of the business to secure their services (and your clients), or offering reduced hours (giving them some security), for example twenty hours per week at $45 per hour as a contractor while they build up their own business. By doing so, the superstar is less likely to pinch your clients (down to loyalty), and can also help train up the new person as well as being there for you if (or when) a backup is ever needed.*

Problem: *one of your incredibly talented female employees is sick of the travel to work and the increasing costs it incurs. The travel time is breaking her emotionally and all she wants to do is move to the country and be a farmer. She has so much experience and has formed such solid relationships with your clients, she is almost irreplaceable.*

Solution: *offer her two 10-hour days per week in town and two days working from her new country farmhouse (via the internet, if possible). You also show her how her superannuation can potentially be used to purchase the farm. If she needs to borrow as well to buy the farm she'll be working, her superannuation fund can also do that. In the meantime, she can keep a small place in the city to live, which will also increase in value over time, providing a hedge in case she hates the part-time country life and wants to return to the big smoke (which happens far* *more often than you'd think). (Flip to my chapter on Farming with Superannuation for more about that).*

Problem: *one of your employees is finding the cost of privately educating their children so worrying that they're only 80% engaged at work. Worse still, you're told they're spending a lot of time searching career sites for a higher-paying job so they can meet the expenses.*

Solution: *sit down and show them how to draw up a budget, put budget deficits into context, and learn to understand them. For example, let's say they are over-spending by $10,000 every year. So what? The value of their home is increasing (or perhaps they have other assets that are appreciating in value that you can identify), their interest payments are cheaper than the equivalent rent, and in three years the spouse will be returning to the workforce in some capacity.*

In the meantime, change the mortgage from principal and interest to interest-only payments (so reducing them), and if that's not possible, why worry about capitalising the debt by $30,000 over three years? Forget about it. Accept it, given it's for only a small window of time before things return to normal. (See the chapter about The Cost of Children for more about this).

I'll stop there, because I can come up with an example from every chapter in this book (and then some). The point is to think outside the box in terms of your own circumstances. Your workers are there for their reasons, not yours, and each of them carries worries and financial distractions of their own.

So start the process. Be the hero.

Engaging them with debt

Prior to the GFC, I once went to a seminar where a group had gathered to discuss ways to hold onto good staff. One of the older members of the group, with many years of experience, offered a way to retain people that had obviously been shaped from just as many years of being burned by staff loss.

His advice was simple: give them a bit of debt.

It was a clever remark, and one that has stayed with me.

Traditional methods to anchor someone to an organisation often involve employee shares or options, but there are plenty of other methods out there.

His comment (which at the time seemed a bit brash) was far from a negative. What better way to show people the measure of their worth to you and to your organisation than by involving them in some way with its finances and success.

For example, the business is about to buy new premises to operate from and you offer your key staff members the option of buying into it with you. Alternatively, let's say you need to purchase a new piece of equipment (or example, a new light truck), and instead of taking out a lease on it, you have a key employee's low (or no) income spouse act as the financier, at a rate a few percent above the personal finance rate (raised against their home, for example), and equivalent to what you would have had to pay for vehicle finance. And if your employee's spouse has a low (or no) income, the profit from the difference is very likely going to be tax free! These are just two examples. If you put your mind to it, dozens of other options are entirely possible.

'Giving them a bit of debt', though, is better phrased as 'giving them a bit of win/win debt' and consider how that goes for their status at work and their financial circumstances. Do you think they'll now leave you quickly, or be less engaged when it comes to ensuring the success of your business?

SUMMING IT ALL UP

Don't hesitate to instigate the process of eliminating your employees' financial distractions. When you do, you create much greater team engagement. Aligning your employees' goals with the desired outcomes for the business is the real key to their retention.

Doing both makes you the hero.

CHAPTER THIRTEEN

LATE TAXES, PENALTIES AND DEBTS

So you haven't lodged a tax return for years? Your GST returns are behind? You owe the tax office money or have been hit with Australian Tax Office (ATO) penalties? Would any or all of these events be financial distractions that could affect the quality of your life?

You bet!

The good thing is that they're one of the easiest distractions to address.

Contrary to popular belief, the ATO is very human and very understanding where there are genuine reasons behind these omissions. And even when the reasons aren't all that genuine, getting in before the ATO chases you down often results in a good outcome, especially when you're dealing with professionals who handle this kind of thing on a regular basis.

I'm pretty sure the ATO's attitude is often (though not always) one of relief that a rogue taxpayer has come back into line, and so it tends to be more forgiving, as opposed to when it has to chase people down (which it will eventually and very rightfully do).

Let's look at a case study to put this in context.

Gary hadn't lodged a tax return for six years. Things had gotten a little mixed up, what with one of his parents dying and his relationship with his wife starting to sour. Gary was falling apart. But then two years had passed and Gary was too disorganised (and just a little bit fearful) to bring his tax affairs back into order.

The guilt and distraction chipped away at Gary, but he just brushed it off, thinking that he normally received refunds anyway. Added to that, he couldn't find all his group certificates and receipts so he could claim his deductions.

Gary just kept putting it off.

Then the ATO sent him a letter. It was a default penalty notice for $3,300 in penalties and back taxes plus interest, which the ATO estimates (in its favour) if you don't lodge within 14 days.

This actually happens a lot.

And what follows is a shameless plug for accountants. The reality is, though, that having a good accountant do your tax return for you (especially given their fees are tax deductible), and who will always know more about maximising allowable tax deductions than you will, is critical for a better result.

In fact, it's almost madness if you're *not* seeing one!

An accountant can also check online and in most recent cases get your group certificates for you (so you don't have to do any of the running around), and can even work within allowable estimation methods to re-create your lost expenses, have your returns lodged quickly to avoid the ATO fines, estimated taxes and interest, and *still* get you a refund.

So dump the distractions of late taxes, penalties and debts. The reality is that if you're holding on to all of that, you're *choosing* to do so!

See a good accountant. Put some money back into your bank account.

If the ATO has applied interest and penalties, and there's a genuine reason behind your failure to comply, let an accountant write an appeal to the ATO on your behalf. You'd be surprised at how many times the ATO comes to the party, because in virtually *every* genuine case, the ATO will actually remit these in full.

In the case where there are debts to the ATO that you can't immediately repay, your accountant will know how to negotiate payment plans to suit, again usually interest free.

It's up to you. Get on top of this ugly financial distraction today.

THE WHOLE POINT

Giving in to financial distraction means you're not set with your vision for the future and your goals.

And taking action about it is entirely up to you. Action–any action–will bring you results.

Taking no action, though, is a choice *you* make.

The aim of this book is to show you *how* to take action (and hopefully that doing so isn't as daunting as you may think), and how to adapt the case studies I've provided to fit your circumstances, or at least to set you to thinking about your own circumstances and to remove the financial distractions from your life.

Aligning your vision and goals with your financial circumstances is essential, and sometimes (as you've seen throughout the book) a lateral or timeline-type focus needs to be employed to do this. In most cases, though, it's not too late to effectively employ most of the strategies I've covered here.

It's up to you now.

Get started yourself or get some professional help.

Nearly everything you need to know is here, so take the time to read it, re-read it and apply it to your own circumstances.

As another step, feel free to subscribe to my bi-monthly newsletter. (Go to **www.financialdistraction.com.au** for more information about how to do that).

Most of all, very best of luck! A life free of financial distraction really is just around the corner!